Early Scottish Angling Literature

Early Scottish Angling Literature

Professor N.W. Simmonds

SWAN·HILL
PRESS

Copyright © 1997 N. W. Simmonds

First published in the UK in 1997
by Swan Hill Press, an imprint of Airlife Publishing Ltd

British Library Cataloguing-in-Publication Data
 A catalogue record for this book
 is available from the British Library

ISBN 1 85310 825 1

Typeset by Hewer Text Composition Services
Printed in England by Livesey Ltd, Shrewsbury

Swan Hill Press
an imprint of Airlife Publishing Ltd
101 Longden Road, Shrewsbury, SY3 9EB, England.

Contents

Foreword

For a long time I have been interested in the early literature of Scottish angling, first fired by the loan of a friend's copy of Stoddart's *The Art of Angling* (1835). The friend and colleague responsible was Angus Macarthur, companion and mentor on many excursions, and I offer him my best thanks and compliments for getting me going. As I looked further, I soon found that there was no coherent, or even comprehensive, account of the subject, only a formidable mass of literature, some of it clearly very good, some of it bad to terrible. On the more positive side, John Waller Hills, in his *History of Fly Fishing for Trout* (1921), clearly recognised the wealth of the nineteenth-century Scottish literature. James Robb in his *Notable Angling Literature* (1947) did the same and gave some very readable quotations, while William Lawrie's *Scottish Trout Flies* (1966) adopted an agreeably historical perspective. Thus incited, I undertook extensive reading, with a view, ultimately, to write upon the subject.

I chose, finally, to limit my enquiries to works on fishing practice up to the end of the nineteenth-century, which meant at least scanning many books by later authors whose experience often went back for decades. So this book is a critique of the published literature rather than a detailed account of how Scottish anglers fished. There is, of course, much on methods and tackle, especially those applied to trout and salmon fishing, which have generated nearly all the literature. Pike, perch, eels and sea fish must have been taken in vast numbers but it was the 'game fish' that drew the leisure anglers and the writers.

I am, therefore, writing about angling and anglers. I exclude pure natural history and fish culture, even though Scotsmen were a leading source of both understanding and management of those important subjects. Thus, interesting as they were, Howietoun (Maitland, 1887) and Stormontfield (W Brown, 1862) make no appearance here.

The major bibliographic sources of reference are well-known but should be cited. They are the *Bibliotheca Piscatoria* (1861) by Westwood and the *Bibliotheca Piscatoria* (1883) by Westwood and Satchell, also the supplement to the latter by R B Marston (1901). An extensive bibliography, which I have not used or tested, is given by Estcourt in *Manchester Anglers' Association* (1883, 1, pp.243ff.). For those interested in Scotland, the most useful work is R J W Coleby's book entitled *Regional Angling Literature* (1979). I am very happy that it was, in part, my enquiries in search of books for my own modest library that provoked Mr Coleby to write this excellent work. I acknowledge with gratitude his help, not only in providing books, but also in offering expert bibliographic guidance. I also acknowledge the valuable help provided by the staff of the National Library of Scotland in finding works and tracking pseudonyms, and from the Edinburgh City Archivist, Mr Richard Hunter, for help with some historical problems on which he brought a happy combination of angling, bibliographical and historical skills. Mr Colin McKelvie's guidance on presentation and selection of anthological material was of much value and I acknowledge it with gratitude

I have tried to present the most complete bibliography possible within the defined area of interest but this book is about angling and I have not aimed at bibliographical profundity. Some editions may be unlisted and I do not pretend to have always sorted out the chaotic mess of dates, titles, reprintings, editings and supplements that characterise much nineteenth-century literature. Very long titles are an abomination and I have ruthlessly shortened them in the text, though they are mostly complete in the bibliography (Franck's title being an exception, of course). In the text, I regularly refer, for brevity's sake, to the *Dictionary of National Biography* and the *National Library of Scotland* by the initials, DNB and NLS.

The reading for this book took years, the drafting but a few weeks. I found, as I wrote, that I had often come to quite decided views on various subjects. I do not mind stating them because an author who has read widely is, I believe, entitled to his opinions. So I admit to being somewhat opinionated and the reader may disapprove if he will: perhaps disapproval may even provoke some to find and read the originals. The anthology appended will, I hope, give some little taste of a fascinating literature.

Acknowledgements

N early all the quotations and illustrations in this book are taken from my own collection; few are subject to copyright. Borrowings and observations on copyright are made as follows, in approximate chronological order. I acknowledge with gratitude permissions from the persons and bodies listed.

(1) The Trustees of the Mitchell Library, Glasgow, for permission to copy J D Dougall's 'Twelve Golden Rules' from *Salmon and Trout Angling* (1841).
(2) The Fishmongers' Company, London, for permission to copy a cover from *The Fishing Gazette* (1893).
(3) The Editor of the *Scots Magazine* and the Editor of the *Flyfisher's Journal*, Mr Kenneth Robson, for permission to use, in a highly edited form, material on T T Stoddart which had already appeared in their journals.
(4) Mr R J W Coleby for permission to copy a quotation from Hicks's (1855) *Wanderings* and a figure of Loch Veyatie from the same work.
(5) Mr Richard Hunter for copies of quotations from Colquhoun (1840–88) and Grimble (1902) and a cover of the *Scots Angler* (1896).
(6) Mr Humphrey Spaight of the Institute of Civil Engineers and Messrs A&C Black for help in trying to trace information about Frederick Fernie. In the event, I quote from his book on *Dry Fly Fishing* (1912) on the assumption that the work is out of copyright. I was unable to trace descendants or relatives of Fernie, despite advertisements on the radio and in the local press.
(7) Mr Peter G Caldwell, great-nephew and only descendant of R C Bridgett, for permission to take several quotations from the excellent works of his great-uncle.

1
Forerunners

The earliest relevant writer was not a Scot but an Englishman and a dull and prosy writer at that. He was Richard Franck (1624–1708). Born in Cambridge, he was a Cromwellian trooper, a religious bigot, a bag of wind and an abominable writer but he was clearly a real angler who fished in Scotland and possessed much knowledge. He lived for many years in Nottingham and thence visited Scotland about 1656–57, apparently mainly touring the Loch Lomond area. There is little evidence that he was widely travelled in Scotland (though C V Bark (1992) suggests otherwise) or that he observed local angling practices with understanding. His book, which he says was written in 1658 but not published until 1694, is best known simply as *Northern Memoirs*, though the full title runs to 15 lines of the DNB (some kind of record, perhaps?). The title page has been reproduced several times (for example by Lamond (1931) and by Bark (1992)). I can see no point in reproducing it again here.

After its fearsome title, *Northern Memoirs* proceeds to 24 pages of blethery dedications, 14 pages of preface and bad verse and only then the work proper, 304 pages (in dialogue form, so help us!), with angling bits scattered among much turgid blether and half-baked moral philosophy. There is a sizeable systematic treatment of fishes, all the usual English ones of course, with no clear Scottish bent except, perhaps, a better description of salmon spawning than was usual at the time. He did do some fly fishing, and advised a bright fly for a dark day, downstream casting and the use of the 'dubbing bag'. He wrote an anti-Walton diatribe, of course, but we must assume, I suppose, that his tackle and methods were almost the same as old Isaak's. Henry Lamond (1931) seems to be almost alone in saying anything kind about this dismal work and its awful author; but even he was not exactly enthusiastic.

Now for two rather obscure little works. First, James Keill, with his *Practical Treatise* (1729), was a mysterious, shadowy figure. I have not seen his work (a mere pamphlet of 16 pages) and have given up trying to find it. It is not in the *Bibliotheca Piscatoria* (1861) by Westwood but appears in the Westwood and Satchell revision of 1883. The NLS index does not list it but collateral evidence (probably slightly shaky!) suggests that the author might have been a Scottish medic practising in the South. The book's publication in Edinburgh seems to be the only reason for regarding it as Scottish.

Second, an only slightly less obscure work, is that of 'Capt. Clarke (RM)', *Angler's Desideratum* (1839), who probably really did write the small book often described as 'anonymous'. It is very rare but the NLS kindly obtained a photcopy for me. It is unclear who Clarke was (he does not appear in the DNB) but it seems possible that he may have been an officer of the Royal Marines. He was evidently wealthy and well-connected, fished the Tweed for trout and salmon, was an excellent practical tackle man and fly-tyer and a thoughtful angler. He invented a 5–6 fly dropperless cast in about 1814 and did well with it on Tweed, fishing the rise whenever possible, especially in calm, bright weather. Some writers (for example, in the *Fishing Gazette*, 1885, 11, pp. 275–6) have sought to describe him as a dry fly pioneer but, I think, there is no real evidence of this. He merely chucked at rising fish, and what sensible trout fisher does not?

The last and most interesting of the significant forerunners is Colonel Thomas Thornton and his entrancing book *Sporting Tour* (1804). The work (which Walter Scott thought 'somewhat tedious') has been through several editions, of which the 1896 version edited by Maxwell is especially attractive. Thornton's life is well documented in the DNB and Michael Brander in his work *Soho for the Colonel* (1961) amplifies the treatment fully and thoughtfully. 'Soho', incidentally, is the hunting cry 'sohowe'. Thornton's father was MP for Stourton, Yorks and the family was clearly wealthy and well-connected. Thornton was born in London in 1757 and died in Paris in 1823 after a picturesque career largely, but not entirely, devoted to field sports.

The book, and especially its title, suggests a single major tour by a vigorous sporting gentleman with a large retinue. In fact, his contact with Scottish sport, especially angling but also shooting and falconry, was spread over many years, at least 1782–94 according to Brander. He made many visits, not simply the one tour, and actually built and owned a Speyside lodge for several years. We are not well informed on his angling techniques but he certainly fished the fly and trolled, on loch and river, had his retinue out netting anything with fins, and regarded 'trimmers' with live-baits (his 'fox-hounds') as a rewarding method of catching pike. When gorge-baiting for pike, incidentally, he believed in deferring the strike. As the dapper for sea-trout is sometimes advised to say 'God Save the Queen' three times, so Thornton thought the pike fisher should read a sermon or a chapter from *Pilgrim's Progress* before lifting his rod.

Thornton caught enormous numbers of fish, some of them large, even huge. Examples include a perch of 7 lb 3 oz from Loch Lomond (along with 150 assorted perch and trout the same day); a huge pike from Loch Alvie, plausibly estimated at 47–48 pounds; three trout in the range 7–9 pounds when trolling the head of Loch Tay; and numerous salmon of about 40 pounds. Maxwell was inclined to doubt Thornton's veracity but Brander (1961) and Lamond (1931) did not and neither do I. How sad that he can not be credited with the UK record perch, as he almost certainly deserves it! Thornton was a man to whom things 'happened', largely as a result of his adventurous habits. He and his retinue suffered storm and flood, hair-raising walks in very rough country, innumerable duckings, wild chases about lochs in leaky boats, defective tackle breakages and so on. On one occasion in Strath Spey, he was nearly skewered by the broken pole of a collapsing tent. On another, at Loch Petulichge (nowadays Petyoulish, near Aviemore), he 'threw in three fox-hounds, lost one and only recovered the other two at the risk of a Highlander's life'. His retinue may have had a rough time but so did Thornton himself; he was certainly 'a man of bottom'.

Thornton was well-connected and wealthy, a welcome guest to many of the lairds of the day. Clearly, he was also good company who loved a bottle or two, a ceilidh and the pipes (the last best heard outdoors, admittedly). Unlike Tom Stoddart, he was no Sassenach snob in his dealings with Highlanders and their ways. Though he and his company often camped, he also used the local inns: the one at Killin was excellent but the preceding one, at 'Cree in la Roche', was not. How, for Heaven's sake, did Crianlarich become so Frenchified? Generally, Thornton's book is a splendid one; it is lively and informative on Scottish fish of the day, without being a how-to-do-it manual. He has been well served by his commentators especially Michael Brander, who well appreciated the qualities of one of the most entertaining fishing books ever written. Brander did a superb job of sorting out Thornton's literary and chronological confusions.

As I remarked above, Walter Scott rather disapproved of Thornton but that may have been a reflection of the fact that Thornton beat him to the draw on what was to become a substantial industry – the romanticisation of the Highlands. Scott only began to exploit this rich literary vein in 1810–14, years after Thornton travelled and wrote. But Our Dear Queen probably read Scott rather than Thornton.

Sir Humphry Davy (1778–1829) fished in Scotland as well as in England but his book is, in my opinion, turgidly worthless (and partly in dialogue form, too). He was an eminent scientist whose main claim to such eminence was that he encouraged Michael Faraday, who was a genius rather than merely an eminent gent. The DNB does not mention fishing but does say that Lady Jane, who came from Kelso, was a bitch, especially to Faraday. Two other writers of marginal interest also deserve reference, if only to justify the inclusion of their titles in the bibliography. They are W Carroll (1818) and T C Hofland (1839). The former wrote a second-rate compendium of flies and fishes and the only Scottish connection is that his book was published in Edinburgh. Hofland (he of 'The Fancy') was an English angling tourist who visited Scotland in 1813 and 1834, but had nothing of real interest to say. His patron was the sculptor, Sir F L Chantrey (1781–1841), also an angler.

2
Thomas Tod Stoddart

Tom Stoddart (1810–80) was the most important and influential of all the earlier writers on Scottish angling. He was not an innovator, and expounded the traditional Scottish angling methods incomparably well and sympathetically from about 1830 onwards. W C Stewart was more important as an influence on angling practice and other nineteenth-century authors expounded the 'nuts and bolts' of angling as well as or better than Stoddart; but none brought the same quiet, devoted good sense and sheer charm to the subject as he did. This chapter is a much-edited version of a piece that appeared in the *Scots Magazine* in 1972 and also in the *Journal of the Flyfishers' Club* in 1994. I am indebted to the editors of both these periodicals for permission to use the material.

Thomas Tod Stoddart qualified in law but never practised. He wrote bad poetry and excellent books about angling and fished from childhood into old age. Many men fish for pleasure and others fish for a living but few have ever lived for fishing with the single-minded devotion that Stoddart brought to the sport. It was in reply to a question from his friend the Sheriff, Henry Glassford Bell, that Stoddart replied: 'Doing? Man, I'm an angler'.

The information we have about Stoddart's life comes from an excellent and sympathetic biography written by his only daughter, Anna M Stoddart, published in 1889 as an introduction to a new edition of his *Angling Songs*. The family came from the Borders: there were 'Stouthearts in Ettrick in 1462'. His father was Pringle Stoddart, a distinguished naval officer of private means and uncertain temper. Thomas, the second child but eldest son, was born in Edinburgh after his father's retirement. It was a great period for building in the city and at least two of the houses the family lived in were swallowed up in the 'spec developments' of the time. The phrase, now pejorative, meant something different in Edinburgh in the early nineteenth-century; 'spec' or not, the New Town was one of the greatest achievements of the human spirit.

It was also a great period intellectually. The University and the Royal Society throve; Scott and Hogg were at the heights of their powers; book and magazine publishing flourished. Indeed, Edinburgh was one of the most civilised cities in the world. It is not surprising that Thomas, a well-educated scion of a prosperous family, dabbled in literature from an early age. Pringle planned a career at the Scottish Bar for his son and as Anna later wrote, 'It is the fate of poetic youths to be bred to the law'.

With law in view, Pringle sent Thomas to Edinburgh University in 1825 but only succeeded in confirming the boy's literary interests. To his lasting good fortune, Thomas fell under the influence of Professor John Wilson, 'Christopher North', then holder of the chair of Moral Philosopy at the University (see Chapter 3). At the Professor's house he met a brilliant group of people, as well as his university classmates and life-long friends, John Wilson Jr and John Aytoun. Pringle, naturally, disapproved, as he also disapproved of his son's growing passion for angling. Paternal objection notwithstanding, Thomas scribbled and fished, abetted in both activities by the Wilson circle who were all writers and nearly all anglers, too.

In 1828, Thomas and his friends, Wilson and Aytoun, made their first excursion to St Mary's Loch and Tibby Shiel's Inn. Tibby was a widow who had, in the manner of the times, reverted to her maiden name; she was evidently something of a character, a superb cook and an excellent hostess to her anglers. As Thomas explains in the *Rambles* (1866) Tibby's place was not really an Inn, and thus she could select her guests, who were clearly a diverse, entertaining, convivial and sometimes eccentric assemblage. It must have been somewhere about this time, aged about 18 years, that Thomas was finally lost to the law and won to angling as a way of life.

His literary endeavours, which he took quite seriously during his undergraduate years, were more productive but hardly more successful than his legal ones. In truth, he was generally a bad poet and, at best, an indifferent one. If Stoddart is remembered at all as a poet, it is for his *Angling Songs* but even these seem to me to be mostly lame pieces, though one was praised by Wilson. His shorter, early poems were gathered under one cover and published by Blackwood. Thereafter he wrote only a few more (published as *Songs of the Seasons* in 1873), and instead, aged 29, he devoted himself to the serious business of the life on which he was already well embarked, namely angling and writing about angling.

There were anglers in Stoddart's family back at least to his grandfather in the middle of the eighteenth-century, and presumably to his forebears in the Borders. Thomas himself fished as a child in and around Edinburgh (as related in the *Rambles*) and on family holidays. By the age of 18, he was evidently a lost man; in 1831 and 1832 he made fishing excursions to the Highlands of Perthshire and Argyll, and started his serious fishing writing in 1833. Besides being a fanatical fisher, he was clearly a formidable walker, as the *Rambles* reveal.

In 1835, he made a long, solitary tour afoot in the north and north-west and there met his future wife, Bessie McGregor, at

17

Contin in Ross-shire. Predictably, his family disapproved, but there must have been a tough streak in Thomas for he held out for marrying his beloved as well as for an angling life. At all events, Pringle Stoddart gave up the struggle, allowed his son a 'small competency' and so set him up as a sort of angling remittance man. The couple were married in 1836, spent a year in the north and in 1837 settled in Kelso, by Stoddart's beloved Tweed.

The 'small competency' was evidently small indeed but the young couple managed on it, with several changes of lodging, until 1848 when the admiral died and they found themselves rather better off. By this time, they had settled in what was to be their permanent home, Bellevue Cottage, Beaumont Street, Kelso. It was here that their children, two sons and a daughter, were born during the period 1838–42. The house no longer stands.

From arrival in Kelso in 1837 until his death in 1880, Stoddart spent over half his life fishing his beloved Border streams: Tweed, Teviot, Ettrick and Yarrow. He did make occasional excursions to other parts of Scotland and even visited London twice, but these were merely minor diversions in a placid routine of Border life and Border angling. Though he caught plenty of Highland trout in his time, he never had much regard for them; indeed, he thought they were rather stupid.

As might be expected of a man of education and modest private means, he took some part in local affairs, gave public lectures, held office in the Tweed and Teviot fishing clubs, and concerned himself in the public debates that led to the 1857 and 1859 Bills regulating fishing in Tweed and the Prevention of Pollution in Rivers Act of 1876. There is nothing especially modern about our contemporary concerns with pollution!

Stoddart had a warm gift of friendship and remained in touch with many of the angling and literary companions of his youth: Wilson, Ferrier, Aytoun, Gordon and others. 'The conversation at Bellevue Cottage did not range over a wide area. There were two absorbing subjects – angling and poetry and angling took the precedence,' Anna later wrote. Professor Wilson died in 1854 and his son, Stoddart's great friend, in 1865. By then, most of his other friends were also dead and Thomas himself was beginning to feel the weight of years. He fished less and less and, in his last decade, was out only one day a week or none at all. In 1877 he caught his last Tweed salmon and never fished again. He died in November 1880, having a few days before walked by his beloved Tweed for the last time. Bessie died in 1885.

If Stoddart's larger literary efforts were disastrous and his short poems indifferent, his angling writing is of another order altogether and can be read with pleasure to this day. Indeed, he was one of the more important British writers of the nineteenth-century on the subject and certainly the first significant Scottish one. His angling writings are important and also abundant. His first book, and perhaps the most important, is *The Scottish Angler*, subtitled *The Art of Angling as Practised in Scotland*. It was based on essays in *Chambers Journal* and published as a book by Chambers in 1835 when the author was 24 years old. A new edition ('greatly enlarged') came out in 1836 and others followed. His next book, *Angling Reminiscences*, was published in Edinburgh in 1837. It is a collection of angling anecdotes in the form of conversations between a group of friends; it is verbose, stilted and of little more than antiquarian interest. Isaac Walton's dialogue form has had many bad followers, several, alas, noted in these pages. His third book is *The Angler's Companion to the Rivers and Lochs of Scotland*, published by Blackwood (1847, second edition, extensively revised, 1853). This is essentially a much amplified version of *The Scottish Angler* and is the most important and certainly the best known of his books. His fourth and last work is *An Angler's Rambles and Angling Songs* (1866), which consists of fascinating reminiscences of angling experiences interspersed with indifferent verses.

In his fishing techniques, Stoddart was a traditionalist, not an innovator. He used the long, heavy rods and horse-hair lines of the time, even though greenheart, built-cane and dressed silk lines were all becoming available before his death. He tied his own flies, of course, and was content with the thinly dressed, sombre patterns of the Tweed. He said that four patterns were enough but had an elastic definition of 'pattern', and obviously used far more. He was not only content with traditional flies but positively disliked anything fancy and even a tinsel rib was to be avoided, though he allowed that it had its uses for tempting stupid Highland fish. His conservatism is well expressed in the following quotation from *The Scottish Angler*, referring to a fancy pattern: 'the latest urban conceit redoubted as a killer, the fail-me-never of some sporting parson or half-pay hero'. 19

He preferred fly fishing to all other forms of angling, and trout to all other forms of fish. But, on occasions, he used worms, maggots, minnows, creepers, parr-tails and even salmon-roe, and he sometimes fished for salmon, sea trout, pike, perch and eels as a diversion from the serious business of catching trout. His instructions on all these are full and explicit and clearly founded on traditional practice, tempered by his own very considerable experience. He mentions an eel estimated at 20 pounds, a record by any standards; and regarded perch as excellent eating (so long as they were fried whole, without de-scaling).

In the *Fishing Gazette* (8 December, 1883, p. 599) there is an interesting note that reveals the existence of an extensive angler's diary. His son, Pringle, had emigrated to Otago, New Zealand where he became President of the Otago Angling Association and active in the introduction of new fish stocks, including Loch Leven trout from Howietoun. He visited Scotland in 1883 and addressed the Kelso Angling Association at a meeting of which he displayed his father's diary and 'literary journal'. The diary records that, over 50 years, he had, in 4,150 days fishing, caught 928 salmon, 1,540 sea trout, 61,573 yellow trout and 378 pike, a total of 67,419 fish in all. Eels and such-like evidently did not count! Presumably, these Stoddart documents still exist somewhere in New Zealand and it would be of great interest to see copies of them lodged somewhere in Scotland. My thanks are due to Richard Hunter for drawing my attention to this reference.

Stoddart was generally against boats, though he agreed that they were useful for trolling lochs; he recommended a large basket, big enough to hold two stone of fish (W C Stewart later used to reckon on ten pounds of trout per day). He believed in 60-pound pike but thought that two-stone ferox belonged to 'roseate fiction'. He thought that river angling was in decline due to land drainage and that Loch Leven was worthless (but then a Tweed man would). He was a hopeless Sassenach in the Scots sense of Saxon (that is, non-Gaelic) and was anti-Highland in almost everything, except that he did allow that the flask and a dram had merits. Thus he held decided views, some of them perhaps mistaken or even a little silly, but what good and prolific writer did not?

Stoddart laboured for the conservation of salmon stocks and played a useful part in promoting the important nineteenth-century legislation on pollution, netting and close seasons. In his earlier years, however, he was prepared to accept, even to engage in, salmon spearing, though not without a certain ambivalence of attitude on the subject. Leistering salmon, he said, was a manly sport (especially for the lower orders of society) and one merely to be discouraged rather than suppressed. He describes a party of local worthies (including James Hogg) assembling at the Gordon Arms for a leistering expedition on the Yarrow. The party moved upstream ('waist-deep in Bridge pool') to the light of torches, brandishing their three-pronged spears. It was 'a gallant chase worth at least fifty fox-hunts' – and at least as hazardous, by the sound of it. The Gordon Arms is still there, an agreeable resort for the homing angler who fancies a pint.

If Stoddart was ambivalent about leistering, he had no doubts about the otter. It was an abomination which he nevertheless described in some detail. It was, he said, an English invention, 'a system in practice in the English Lakes and gradually creeping northwards'. We do not have to believe this and, for my part, I suspect that Stoddart was shifting moral obloquy for an invention that the Scots were perfectly capable of achieving for themselves (and had far more places in which to practise the art).

From his descriptions of tackle (especially of plaited horse-hair lines) and from miscellaneous inferences from his writings, it seems that Stoddart fished his flies downstream by a sort of switch-casting process, though this is never, I think, quite explicit. His great contemporary, William C Stewart, was in no doubt that this was wrong and said so, loudly and often (Chapter 6). There has been a recurrent suggestion in the literature that Stoddart swished his flies around in the air before casting and that he was therefore an early dry fly fisher. I do not believe it, even if he did remark that trout sometimes rose at the moment when the flies arrived. Though Stoddart and Stewart were both Border traditionalists in a sense, there seems to have been little affinity between them. Perhaps we might say that Stoddart was a devoted angler while Stewart was a fanatic? I know of no evidence that they met but it seems improbable that they did not. Wilson and Stoddart (according to Anna) used to refer to 'The Pretender' after Stewart's book was published and had been well received.

An angling competition, Wilson and Stoddart versus Stewart and Russel (then editor of *The Scotsman* and a fine fisher), was to have

21

taken place at St Mary's Loch but, apparently, never did. Clearly, there was some rivalry between Stoddart and Stewart, which is hardly surprising, but the differences did not go very deep, for both expounded the same general approach to trouting based on traditional Border methods.

I have said that Stoddart laboured long and productively for the conservation of Scottish salmon stocks. This interest was firmly founded in an exceptionally good understanding of the biology and life-cycle of the salmon and its relatives. If we recall that he was writing at a time when even the connections between parr, smolt and salmon and between trout, sea trout and other trout were generally uncertain, then his consistent good sense and substantial accuracy are even more remarkable. Stoddart and Professor John Wilson made some good jibes against Robert Knox, the notorious anatomist, angler and receiver of bodies from Burke and Hare. Some agreeably acerbic exchanges followed.

To conclude, Stoddart was by far the most important figure in early Scottish angling literature, indeed he was one of the most significant authors in the history of trout fishing. He was a good and prolific author, though a poor versifier; a very experienced and successful fisher; a traditionalist in temperament and practice; a minor public figure who laboured well for the general good of Scottish angling; and a 'weel-kent' figure much loved by his many friends.

3
The Wilsons

There are only two Wilsons of any interest for this book but they were both prolific writers. Editions and bibliographies are confused and it does not help that the DNB contains many J Wilsons of the right period. The basic biographical fact is that John Wilson, a successful manufacturer of Paisley, had two sons. The elder son, John (1785–1854), was mostly literary but with angling friends and interests, while the second son, James (1795–1856), was a scholarly natural historian and a devoted angler. Both are reasonably treated in the DNB and there is also a large and exceedingly dull memoir of John Wilson by his daughter, Mary Gordon (1862–1879), evidently an act of family piety and of no angling interest at all. Crombie's short biography in *Modern Athenians* (1882) is a good deal more readable but few writers take him seriously as an angler.

John Wilson was born in Paisley in 1785 and died in Edinburgh in 1854. He read classics at Glasgow and also studied at Magdalene College, Oxford (1803–04). Somewhat mysteriously, he lived in Cumberland from 1808 but somehow collected a Glasgow MA in 1810, read Scottish law and became an Edinburgh Advocate in 1814–15. However, the law was not his *métier* (any more than it was Stoddart's), so he settled to a life of good fellowship and literary journalism. He was editor of the then new *Blackwood's Magazine* ('*Maga*') in 1816–18. In 1820, he succeeded Dr Thomas Brown in the Chair of Moral Philosophy at Edinburgh University, retiring in 1852 in ill health, shortly before his death and subsequent burial in the Dean Cemetery in 1854. (W C Stewart cannot have been buried too far away, nearly 20 years later.) The DNB states that Wilson's appointment to the Chair was 'improper' but that, as a good teacher, though a shaky scholar, the University might have done worse. In retrospect, it cannot have been easy to reconcile University duties with journalism, angling and an evident fondness for convivial company.

As a journalist, he wrote many reviews of books relevant to angling over the period 1823–43, covering works by Walton, Oliver,

Stoddart, Shaw, Young and Scrope. There were also long, post-humous reviews of books by Colquhoun and Young. There may have been more because I have not searched *Blackwood's Magazine* exhaustively. Those essays I have read (most of the above) seem to be windy and egotistical, more relevant to Wilson's interests than to the books themselves. Far more interesting were the chatty essays collected in *Maga* in 1822–35 under the general title '*Noctes Ambrosianae*'. Many were by Wilson himself but anonymity and authorship have never been properly established (as if they mattered!). The best source seems to be Blackwood's 1854 edition in four volumes, allegedly the first UK collection. Some (probably shaky) scholarship pruned 71 pieces to 39 and the product is readable or, at least, eminently 'dippable'; I doubt if anyone now would have the nerve to read the lot (but the US Eng.Lit. Ph.D. industry is now involved so who knows what might happen?). Much later (1888), there was the 'popular edition', further pruned of transient material and the more readable for that. So the '*Noctes Ambrosianae*', which must have been marvellous reading to knowledgeable Edinburghians ('Athenians') of the day, have come down in the world and are never likely to make a modern mark.

The heart of the *Noctes* was a coterie of friends who met at an imaginary Ambrose's Tavern, the scene of a bloody murder in 1819, supposedly near what is now Register House in the very heart of the city. Conversation in the pub was lively and anecdotal and in Scottish rather than the slightly Scottified English usual among the upper crust of the day; Gaelic was, of course, the preserve of the northern barbarians, not to be admitted to polite society. To confuse the *Noctes* still further, pseudonyms were generally used. John Wilson was 'Christopher North'; James Hogg (one of the greatest of Scottish authors) was 'The Ettrick Shepherd' or, more usually, simply 'Shepherd'; Robert Syme W S (1750–1844) was 'Tim Tickler' (and, incidentally, John Wilson's uncle). James G Lockhart (1794–1850, friend and biographer of Scott), James Ferrier (1808–64, a genuine philosopher and nephew of John Wilson) were also sometimes of the company. The friends not only met and talked but also wandered and fished together. Incidentally, Thomas Tod Stoddart's great friend, John Wilson, was the son of 'The Professor' who was, 'Christopher North', John Wilson Sr, Stoddart's near-contemporary at the University.

THE

ROD AND THE GUN

BEING

TWO TREATISES

ON

ANGLING AND SHOOTING.

BY

JAMES WILSON, F.R.S.E.

AND BY

THE AUTHOR OF

"THE OAKLEIGH SHOOTING CODE."

Stoddart held his friend in very high regard as an angler, as appears in numerous passages in the *Rambles*. They walked all over Scotland together and Wilson held the Dochart around Luib in especially high regard for trouting, fishing there shortly before his death. But Wilson, so far as I can discover, though he contributed much to the good company, contributed nothing to the angling literature.

As I remarked earlier, the company were talkative anglers but the *Noctes* contain little of interest on fishing as such. In my opinion, the best writings are some attributed to 'Shepherd' and a splendidly libellous attack on Robert Knox (see Chapter 7) who allegedly did (and knowingly) receive bodies from Burke and Hare. Knox got away with it but the Edinburgh press and mob did not think he should have done so and nearly lynched him. Anyway, Knox, a disagreeable fellow, made some nasty jibes at members of the *Noctes* circle and deserved no sympathy. As to Hogg, he was a superb writer and his Scotticisms are well represented by, for example, playing a

25

fish 'loup, loup louping intil the air, describing in the spray the rinnin rainbows' and 'ministers aye fish for the pot and the gutsy weans'.

The younger brother, James Wilson (1795–1856) was a serious natural historian, a Fellow of the Royal Society of Edinburgh and a worthy but dull writer, far less entertaining than 'Christopher North' and his friends. He was educated at school and University in Edinburgh, travelled widely in Europe from 1816 and settled in Edinburgh to pursue his natural history studies. Presumably he was sustained by family wealth, because he was able to decline the offer of the Chair of Natural History in succession to Forbes in 1854. He made many scientific excursions in 1841–50 (for example, with Sir Thomas Dick Lauder to study herring). He was certainly a practising angler but his writings in the *Encyclopedia Britannica* (1842) and his book, *The Rod and the Gun* (1840–1844) were not exciting. They seem to me to be largely derivative, from such writers as Bainbridge, Salter and Yarrell. Angling, alas, has a long history of plagiarism. Wilson was clearly a fly fisher who denied any idea of exact imitation, remarking that the Wilson family especially favoured the following flies: the Professor (mallard and yellow, but I am still not clear who invented the name), Green Mantle (mallard and green), Long Tom, Sam Slick (was this not re-invented by the rezzermen a few years ago?), Grizzly King (which sounds American) and Fysche Palmer. But the family fancies did not stop him from citing long lists of other people's fail-me-nevers.

So the Wilsons were prominent and early enough to merit a short chapter here but they can hardly be said to have had a major influence on Scottish angling history. However, that history would have been poorer without them.

4
John Colquhoun

ohn Colquhoun of Luss (1805–85) wrote one very fine book and several minor ones. He was son of Sir James Colquhoun, Baronet of Luss and had one of the great Sir John Sinclairs of Caithness as a grandfather. The DNB biography is usefully supplemented by an autobiographical introduction to the seventh and last edition of his major book, *The Moor and the Loch* (1888). Colquhoun went to Edinburgh High School and University and then served in the army until 1834 (with much sporting as well as military activity). He married in 1834, left the army and devoted the rest of his life to sport, with shooting perhaps taking precedence over angling. However, he did remark that angling was a science, shooting 'a mere art', a somewhat ambiguous statement, perhaps. He lived in England but spent a large part of each year in Scotland and was clearly a keen and competent naturalist as well as a skilful sportsman.

His first and most important book, with a terrible long Victorian title which I shall abbreviate to *The Moor and the Loch*, appeared in 1840 and, on its own, is of no great interest since it is dominated by shooting. Later editions were better and the seventh (1888, post-humous) had a shorter title and a vastly enhanced treatment of fishing. Even so, the first two-thirds of the book and all the illustrations are about shooting, and Scottish angling is covered in the last ten chapters, 24–33. Salmon angling (chapters 24–27) receives most attention but Colquhoun was not a narrow specialist because these chapters are followed by writings (chapters 28–33) on, respectively, trolling for ferox, river trouting, burns, loch fishing, salt water lochs and an anecdotal 'Raid on Sutherland', enhanced by lots of big ferox.

For river salmon, Colquhoun favoured a long line, hand-lining on retrieve and shooting line on casting, a single fly reduced in size for low summer water, and 'winding over' (also known as 'backing up'). But he would spin, troll or dangle a bunch of worms on occasion. 27

Since he is one of the earliest really devoted salmon anglers on record, it is interesting that he fished through the summer, with small flies; the more recent literature sometimes leaves the impression that Scottish salmon fishing was a brutal business of dragging huge flies through icy spring and autumn floods – it was not that way for Colquhoun! He has many pleasing anecdotes, showing much experience, remarking, for example, that locally, 'the underhanded upstream throw is much in use' (for example, on the Ness). But he thought it ungainly and unsportsmanlike because it needed a 'strong, clumsy rod'; so much for Spey casting, which, I presume, is what he refers to. He tied his own flies but, alas, gives no details; he seems to have favoured sombre patterns and was very insistent on small sizes in summer. He appears to have disapproved of the 'double-hooked, gaudy and very expensive flies, the present favourites on Tweedside', used there for harling and on Loch Tay for trolling. On the loch, he preferred the cast fly to trolling because it was less disturbing to the fish and, anyway, fish had definite lies. The logic is hardly clear.

Salmon were Colquhoun's favourites. He was the earliest really serious Scottish writer on the subject and had the good fortune to indulge his passion almost endlessly. He even remarked that the trout angler should 'be advised to get out of this nursery fishing, to be a salmon angler if he can and he will be the first to acknowledge its vast superiority'. Later chapters, however, reveal him as a competent trouter, too. Perhaps he should be compared with his near-contemporary, Tom Stoddart, each devoted to one fish but prepared to chase the other on occasion. Colquhoun chased trout on rivers, burns and lochs by all the usual methods. On the river he favoured the general Border style of the day, threw at the rise if he could (who does not?), fished the deeps carefully and dressed himself darkly in the 'slate blue of the heron's back'. On the burn, he wormed upstream in clear, low water. On the loch, he waded the shore, trolled for ferox (very successfully) and was prepared to drift worms or a gorge bait on a float to catch anything that would eat the offering. He also described 'trimmers', constructed around well-corked bottles, presumably for pike (though the odd ferox probably did not come amiss).

Finally, and unusually for the writers of his day, he fancied fishing sea lochs for anything that swam: when trolling for sea trout (but not salmon, of course), the handline, a set of 3–4 rods carrying feathers, and the 'long line' were all useful on occasion. If one hooked something large on the feathers, one simply chucked the rod overboard to fish for itself; did not Walton also recommend something like this for large trout? The long line, with 300–600 hooks, was declining in effectiveness and was used less frequently after the mid-century. Colquhoun clearly enjoyed the practice but wrote that 'there is generally so much filth and discomfort in the whole business that gentlemen seldom care to engage in it'; gentleman or no, he clearly loved it.

The only other mid-century Scottish writer I know of who took sea-fishing seriously was Christopher Idle whose excellent book *Hints on Shooting and Fishing* (1855) (see Chapter 7) was contemporary with Colquhoun. There are many points of similarity, of course, but I detected no evidence of plagiarism (all too common in the angling literature).

Colquhoun's earlier books (1849, 1858, 1866) are readable but unremarkable. Many passages recall *The Moor and the Loch*, even to verbatim identity of substantial sections. It is my impression that he stitched many parts of all four books together in the later editions of *The Moor and the Loch* and that his fishing style and practices did not change much from the 1840s onwards. He wrote agreeably enough, but his literary stitching was a bit careless and the seams tended to show. But he was surely an important writer and good to read, even now, well over a century later.

5
William Scrope

William Scrope (1772–1852) was the 'last of a line' of Wiltshire gentlemen, son of a parson, a classical scholar, a competent amateur painter, a field sportsman, a lively writer, a bit of an eccentric but, above all, a salmon fisher. He came to the sport late, aged·about 50 but then spent some 20 years (1823–43) by the Tweed, with occasional excursions to other parts of Scotland: he mentions the Ness, Loch Shiel and south-western rivers in passing, but no more.

His one book, *Days and Nights of Salmon Fishing in the Tweed*, appeared in 1843, when he was 70 and just leaving Scotland to spend his last ten years in the south. There was a posthumous second edition (1854) and, much later, H T Sheringham's attractive third edition of 1921. This is one of the truly great books on angling. It is readable, lively, opinionated, with frequent agreeable tinges of the author's genial eccentricity. I have long felt that Thornton and Scrope had much in common, besides being fanatical emigrés.

Scrope explains that he was contemptuous of London angling and yearned to be 'a real scientific fly fisher'. When dining with friends in London about 1822, he decided to visit Scotland, caught a five-pounder in the Ettrick and was a lost man. In the next 20 years, living at Melrose, he became a friend of Walter Scott, fished endlessly and seemingly fitted well into the local scene because he acquired an exhaustive knowledge of salmon poaching, evidently by practising all the useful techniques in company with the local villains. He was a competent naturalist and his views on the biology of the local salmonids were essentially sound. He knew about parr–smolt–salmon relations by 1825 and keenly followed Shaw's pioneering studies. However, he still believed that bull trout were different from sea trout and, indeed, caught a 16-pounder.

As a fly fisher for salmon (he also spun and wormed), Scrope used the traditional huge rod and about 120 yards of tapered line (what it was made of we are, tantalisingly, not told). Casting, he thought, was 'a knack that cannot be well taught but by experience'. As to flies, he remarked that 'there is no month in the year when salmon flies are made by nature, so no distinction need be observed'. He rather disapproved of flashy fancies (Irish habits had yet to penetrate) but was willing to adapt size and colour to the state of the water. His six favourites (figured in the third edition) would, I think, never be seen today: Kinmont Willie, Lady of Mertoun, Toppy, Michael Scott, Meg with the Muckle Mouth, Meg in her Braws, all enchanting names and, though we know Kinmont Willie from the ballad, who was Meg? Maybe she was the Black Meg of Darnwick who gave her name to Meg's Hole in Tweed above Melrose Bridge?

Scrope seems to have been an energetic fisher, given to hazardous wading. He advised the use of heavy, nailed shoes (with holes to allow drainage) and avoidance of rocking stones; one should not go beyond the fifth waistcoat button and should be careful if one's legs turned black or purple (red was alright). Scrope appears to be a very truthful man, as are all anglers, of course. In 20 years he must have caught thousands of fish but never, he said, one over 30 pounds and few over 20. If one hooked a big fish, he said, it was wise to send one's 'gilly' to bring dinner and supper to sustain the angler during the struggle. It does not sound as though he subscribed to the minute-a-pound rule.

It is hard to avoid the impression that he enjoyed poaching as much as legitimate angling. At all events, he devotes three substantial chapters to the subject, wherein every useful technique (except poisoning) is described. He writes: 'If I were to write an account of half the poaching tricks that are common to all salmon rivers, I should produce a book the dimensions of which would terrify the public, even in this pen-compelling age'. Perhaps we should recall that he was a friend of his neighbour, Walter Scott, and made a jeer at the Professor (clearly Wilson), both of them definite pen-compelled scribblers. He is slightly apologetic about poaching but wrote: 'catch as many salmon as you can, *recte si possis, si non, quocunque modo*'. The Latin justifies the leister, it seems! His methods included: the five-pronged leister or waster for throwing and stabbing; sunning (whereby fish were disturbed in low water by dangling a bleached horse skull over their noses); trolling (for Scrope this meant a cross-line operated from both banks); burning torches (accompanied by leistering); the use of rake-hooks (leaded snatch-hooks which might now be called Walkerburn Angels, I believe); harling also appears in a chapter on poaching, a method that some would now call fly fishing but which Scrope regarded as 'a most prodigiously stupid method of proceeding and little superior to setting night lines'.

During Scrope's time on the Tweed, there were many Scottish anglers and the beginnings of a great surge in angling writing. It is curious, therefore, that Scrope, apart from a jeer at Wilson (who was a literary gent rather than a serious angler), simply does not mention his contemporaries: Stoddart, Younger, Colquhoun and others all published significant books by 1840 but get no mention. Maybe Scrope, though a highly literate man, simply did not read his contemporaries or maybe his devotion to salmon and to poaching isolated him from his predominantly trout-fishing brethern? He sometimes refers to himself as 'Harry Otter' which is strangely reminiscent of the nicknames assigned by John Wilson ('Christopher North') at much the same time to characters in the '*Noctes Ambrosianae*' (see Chapter 3). Scrope had met 'Shepherd' (James Hogg) and had evidently clashed with his 'stiff and bristly opinions'.

6
William Clouston Stewart

W illiam Clouston Stewart (1832–72), is one of the most important Scottish angling writers, not because he was prolific or an innovator (he was neither) but because he lucidly and systematically expounded an approach to trout angling in the Tweed and smaller Border waters that became widely regarded as authoritative. The little that is known about his life has been ably summarised by Richard Hunter in the 1996 facsimile edition of *The Practical Angler* published by the Fly Fishers' Classic Library. Stewart lived in Edinburgh (a tea merchant according to 'Helvellyn' in the *Fishing Gazette*, 1890, 20, pp. 204–5). He died young, of smallpox, aged only 40, wrote one important book, *The Practical Angler* (1857 and later) and had a gift for controversy which was, unfortunately, but little used. *The Scotsman* obituary is useless for facts and the lack of notice in the DNB is, as John Waller Hills said, scandalous. So we are very lucky to have Richard Hunter's research and the only good photograph extant to accompany it.

Stewart was a devoted, even fanatical, angler who had little time for fancy tricks or purple prose; he simply set out to catch trout, lots of them, by fly if possible, by bait or spinning if not. (He clearly had something of Scrope's attachment to sheer achievement.) He said that any competent Border angler should take ten pounds of fish per day and he had a reputation for doing so, by sheer dogged determination, if necessary; one writer remarked that a day out with Stewart was 24 hours of creeping and crawling. He must have known of Tom Stoddart and his friends but they may not have met. They were older than Stewart, given to blether and poesy, did not mind catching salmon and seemed to have regarded him with at least mild disapproval. Perhaps he was just a little too fanatical, even for them; they called him The Pretender. Thus, Stewart seems to have been something of a loner, a solitary fisher who, however, warmly expressed his indebtedness to James Baillie (1815–46) whom he described as 'the ablest fly fisher in Scotland from whom we have received valuable information in that branch of the art'. C V Bark (1992) also noted this indebtedness to Baillie. However great his attachment to the wet fly, he sometimes bent his principles a little, for example, in advocating the use of 'drag-hooks' trailing behind the minnow, a practice that might nowadays be regarded with some dubiety.

What Stewart advocated is well-known and needs no more than a very brief summary. He said that the fly fisher should fish a relatively short, stiff rod, a heavy dressed silk line, small lightly dressed spider flies with soft hackles and throw a short line upstream at all times. The last item was crucial: trout lie with their heads upstream, so the angler coming up quietly from below would be less visible, would present the flies tumbling down naturally and would maximise his chances of hooking a fish by striking downstream at any check or touch. Other anglers (for example, James Dougall and John Younger – see Chapter 7) had taken the general point but none had advocated the practice so plainly and forcibly as Stewart. However, even Stewart admitted that he would chuck short quick casts up and across a large stream if wading deeply, but regarded this as a concession to *force majeure*.

Stewart, of course, had numerous ardent, and sometimes voluble, followers, many of them identified in later chapters. But downstream angling is often easier and less tiring (even with modern tackle) and many fishers have remained unconverted, even to the present day. A good short, pro-Stewart essay was written by J O Mackenzie (*Manchester Anglers' Association*, 1882, 2, pp. 30–43). But that appeared many years after the Master had spoken, when few doubted the principle but many failed to practise it. Stewart was a devoted stream fisher but did occasionally fish still waters – of which he was rather contemptuous. Border anglers necessarily tended to be stream-fishers, of course.

There was no suggestion that Stewart fished the floating fly and J W Hills is correct, I am sure, in saying that he did not invent upstream fishing, though he was surely the most thorough early proponent of it. Hills, incidentally, appears to have been confused about Tom Stoddart's habits, referring to him as an 'upstreamer' in one passage and a 'downstreamer' later; he also wanted to make him a dry fly man (just silly, I think) and assumed that he must therefore have read Pulman's book, because no mere Scot could have invented the art as early as the mid-nineteenth century.

Stewart also wrote a sensible, pithy essay on *Fly Fishing and How it Should be Done* (with content as didactic as its title) in Pennell's book *Fishing Gossip* (1866). His only other work of consequence is *A Caution to Anglers* (1871). It is rare but well worth finding and reading, because it presents a controversy with H C Pennell in a way that makes one regret that he did not dip his pen in vitriol more often. The argument went back to Pennell's use of the title *The Modern Practical Angler*, despite a request to Pennell's publisher not to do so. There followed an acrid exchange of letters in *The Field*, starting with an upstream/downstream controversy, accusations of plagiarism and untruthfulness, and going on to hook shapes, fly patterns and worming rigs; it also included a challenge to Pennell (a 'downstreamer') to outfish an 'upstreamer' of Stewart's choice for a 'considerable sum to charity'. In truth, alas, it was all a bit of a storm in a teacup. Pennell said that many angling books had 'Practical' in their titles so what was Stewart fussing about? Stewart said that Pennell took the downstream practice as best because it was commonest among the ignorant whereas he, Stewart, took it as evidence of laziness or stupidity. Finally, the editor of *The Field* stopped the exchange and Stewart made a few unpublished digs: 'Assertion is not argument and impertinence is not proof' and Pennell's book was a 'compound of plagiarism, absurdity and self-conceit' which would be improved by 'deleting more of what is original and substituting borrowed information' (borrowed, that is, from a reliable source such as – surprise! surprise! – *The Practical Angler*).

Perhaps I over-emphasise the controversy a little because, in truth, there is not much one can usefully say about Stewart: his life and personality are almost unknown and his doctrines are familiar to all. At times, he does seem rather like the prickly Scot putting the arrogant Southerner in his place and maybe that is how it was. Certainly, Pennell deserved to be squelched but Stewart did seem a bit rough; however, he died very soon afterwards and perhaps illness sharpened his bad temper.

Even now, Stewart's doctrines are observed more in principle than in practice and what habitual 'upstreamer' does not bend his methods to the exigencies of wind or water or even a tired wrist?

7
Mid-nineteenth century

n this chapter I shall look at diverse writers who published in, roughly, the 1840s and 1850s. All are interesting but, in my opinion, none is so interesting as to justify a chapter to himself. I have treated them alphabetically, providing a paragraph or two apiece and do the same in Chapter 8 for the latter part of the century.

J G Bertram's book, *The Border Angler* (1858), followed that of W C Stewart by only a year, and was written by Bertram even though it appeared anonymously. It is, frankly, a guide book and the full title suggests promotion of railway interests to English visitors. For trout fishing he drops names continuously: Stewart, Stoddart, David Robertson (also of Kelso) and James Baillie of Lauder ('probably the best fly fisher in the world' – in a inflated echo of Stewart, perhaps?). Baillie, he said, was an 'upstreamer' who taught Stewart the art. Bertram's practical paragraphs are clearly derivative; he added that larger flies (but not Highland gaudies!) would do on St Mary's Loch and that the otter was acceptable, if conscience allowed.

Robert Blakey is a much more substantial figure. An Englishman born in Morpeth in 1795, he lived for many years at Greenock (about 1850 onwards) and died in London in 1878. There is quite good information about him available in a memoir that prefaced William Senior's 1898 edition of Blakey's best book. Blakey also wrote under the pseudonym 'Palmer Hackle'. He was of poor family and largely self-taught, wrote a book about a fishing tour in France and Belgium, became Professor of Metaphysics and Logic at Queen's College, Belfast and from there moved to Greenock, whence came much of his angling writing. He clearly wrote from personal experience in Scotland and elsewhere, but reads more like a professional scribbler than a serious angler. His one serious book is *Angling or How to Angle and Where to Go* (1854–1898) and is worth reading but the rest is mostly weak, second-hand material marred by much name dropping. The editor of the *Fishing Gazette*, presumably to fill in some spare space, borrowed a lot of dull quotations from 'Palmer

Hackle' in 1897–8, wondering who the author really was (cf Chapter 11).

David Cairncross, born in Forfarshire, was a keen angler and naturalist, self-taught and a little eccentric. Eels were bred from beetles according to the frontispiece of his book *The Origins of the Silver Eel* (1862). Most of this unusual book, though, is devoted to trout fishing, using fly, lure and bait fished on sundry curious tackles from a long, even gigantic, rod. It is an agreeable book but not one to be taken too seriously; the life cycle of the eel was only discovered decades later and David Cairncross was not much more in error than most writers over the preceding millenia.

James Dalziell Dougall wrote a good practical angling book entitled *Salmon and Trout Angling* (1841) that describes traditional practices and tackle much like those of Tom Stoddart. He evidently had some Irish experience and remarked that Irish rod ferrules were sometimes fitted 'upside down' to minimise the entry of rain into the joint, an observation more readily regarded, I think, as an Irish joke than as a contribution to tackle design. He fished fly, of course, but minnows, worms and roe were also acceptable, though the last was, perhaps just a little too effective on a large treble in a pool that had been adequately ground-baited. There is a hint of upstream casts fished downstream but the 1841 text is not really clear. His 1861 book, *Scottish Field Sports* (I assume that James D Dougall is the same writer), was post-Stewart and mostly rather bad. He did, however, insist on short, quick, upstream throws, aimed above the water, saying that this had been accepted practice 'time out of mind'. Had it, one wonders, or was Dougall really being wise only after the Stewart event?

Although Adam Dryden called his book *Hints to Anglers* (1862), it is a thorough Border text on fly, worm, minnow, creeper and roe. He was a post-Stewart 'upstreamer' except in winter or very early in the season. He knew the Forth, Clyde and Tweed systems and the (then early) Edinburgh reservoirs, such as Threipmuir, Harlaw, Harperrig and Cobbinshaw. He seemingly had little cause to boast of monsters but says he caught nearly 5,000 trout weighing 860 pounds in February–June 1858. He beat William Stewart's standard ten-pounds-per-outing but his average weight was an unblushing 2.8 ounces. An interesting historical sidelight is that he provides several maps of Border waters in which railways are shown, at that time the standard means of access to fishing. In one, no fewer than five companies are named; 1862 long preceded British Rail but perhaps the multiplicity of lines foreshadows the chaos now being re-visited upon the unfortunate traveller in Britain?

James Hicks is of interest because he forsook the well-trodden Border track for wilder places in the North and West. He travelled from Glasgow by boats and coaches to the Great Glen, Inverness, Lairg and Assynt. (A few years later, in the 1860s, he could have done some of his travelling by train.) He had planned to go on to Rhiconich and the Dionard but did not and, instead, undertook the long walk back to the Great Glen, Rannoch and Loch Lomond. There is much anecdote in his book *Wanderings* but Hicks does not write well and can hardly be said to illuminate the local fishings he sampled. He used Highland-style flies, was not too discouraged by bright calm, took a dim view of innkeepers who overcharged for salmon fishing and then grabbed the fish. *Tout ça change?* He seems to have most enjoyed his stay in and around Altnacealgach (as so many of his successors did until recent years, when the inn burned down). He had some large bags of trout, mostly in the 2–5 fish per pound range. Like so many of the later fishers, he reached Urigil by boat across Borralan and walking ('wet, boggy and extremely irksome'); he liked little Loch Awe and the Gillaroo loch and did well in the burns and wee rivers of the district. A circuit of Urigil was 'a business requiring health, strength and endurance': no doubt. He clearly knew the ground intimately and must have been a tough walker.

Christopher Idle is a rare bird among nineteenth-century writers on Scottish angling. In his book *Hints on Shooting and Fishing* (1855), he devotes two-thirds to shooting but the one-third on fishing is almost entirely about the sea. Of other authors, only John Colquhoun took sea fishing seriously and he devoted but a single, short, tail-piece chapter to it. So Idle is interesting, clearly very experienced and readable, too. He appears English and published in London but was in Scotland a great deal.

He mostly operated from boats with strong local help and used anything from a hand-line-with-paternoster, to multiple rods dragging feathers for saithe and lythe, to the use of 'curtain' and 'bag' nets, and long-lining for anything from haddies to conger and skate. He also fly-fished and trolled for trout in lochs but rather fancied the otter and argued a public duty to remove small trout thus. He barely mentions salmon and seems to have had little interest in them. As to sea fish, he said that lythe ('leith') were also called 'rock whiting', and that saithe ('seithe') were not so good to eat but grew large and were then favoured for salting by poorer people under the name 'stein-loch'. (Colquhoun used the same word as 'stanlock'.)

Robert Knox (1791–1862) was an Edinburgh man, a fine anatomist and teacher but a rather disagreeable person. He was a serious biologist but completely misinterpreted the biology of the salmonids (as the Stoddart–Wilson school happily pointed out). He patronised Burke and Hare, was nearly lynched by the Edinburgh mob (which was rather given to such activities), and was savaged by John Wilson in *Blackwood's Magazine* but exonerated (though only just) by a medical committee protecting its own. He died in London after six years of practice there, having made Edinburgh too hot to hold him. His one angling book, *Fish and Fishing* (1854), is a confused mess of travel, angling and pseudo-science. It is further marred by snobbish name dropping but enlivened by a sneer at Hogg's boozy friends, the *Noctes* circle, a 'vile crew of scribblers' writing 'malicious monthly filth', which nonsense provoked Christopher North's lethal attack on Knox's medico–legal morals. Knox was a villain and received the worst of it, but I confess to a certain sympathy for his sneer at Sir Humphry Davy as the 'mawkish claret-sipping author of *Salmonia* who never said a clever thing in his life'. Davy was, indeed, a dull dog on angling matters, but it is hard to see why Knox so disapproved of claret-sipping, a good old Edinburgh custom, after all; he could not have lived in Edinburgh for years and not drunk a few gallons of it himself.

James Locke grew up fishing around Edinburgh (about 1810). His book *Tweed and Don* (1860) is a confused and ill-constructed but agreeable work. It contains interesting asides to the effect, for example, that the upstream idea was current by 1825 and that Tweedside woollens made their name and mark about 1830. He moved north to Aberdeenshire and records excursions there and to the Spey, Ness, Findhorn, Tay, Glenfinnan and Loch Eil. Latterly, he lived near London and fished rather widely. A practical point about the Spey emerges: as in Ireland, salmon casting lines were made of whip cord (was it linen or hemp?) treated with oil and wax, which sounds superior to the hair or silk and hair mixtures still current in the Borders.

Moffat's book, *The Secrets of Angling* (1865), is a very solid, careful, well-constructed work, an admirable how-to-do-it manual of yesteryear which would not have given Tom Stoddart pause but manages completely to ignore William Stewart's doctrines of nearly a decade before. Besides what one might call 'conventional' fishing, he has some interesting suggestions on unusual baits, ground-baiting, float-fishing, the use of 'trimmers' for trout and even on cookery. I have heard of potted char and eaten potted shrimps but do not recall reading directions for preparing potted trout anywhere else.

The bibliography of John Robertson is confusing. There seems to have been a *Trout Fisher's Manual* which I have not seen. His two books listed here, *Angling Streams* (1859) and *The Handbook of Angling* (1861), are conventional workings of traditional Border practices, except that he first inclines to and later simply promotes the Stewart upstream doctrine. He obviously knew the Tweed Forth, Clyde and Solway waters quite well but numbered catches in dozens of tiddlers and allowed that pounders were uncommon. He also has what appear to be well-informed remarks on the introduction of grayling into south-western Scotland in 1855–57.

John Younger (1785–1860) was one of the 'characters' of Scottish angling but hardly a weighty writer on the subject. He was the village cobbler of St Boswells, 'the Tweedside gnostic' (DNB), a self-taught literary man who had a rather complicated private life, tried village postmastering but returned to cobbling, despised the rich and died 'very poor but honest' (DNB) in 1860. He was, according to his book, *River Angling for Salmon and Trout* (1840, 1864), explicitly an 'upstreamer', used few patterns, knew that water flies did not 'fall' but hatched from 'maggots', used a huge two-handed rod and claimed phenomenal salmon casts (30 yards). On salmon flies, he liked the traditional sombre Tweed patterns and thought they were 'really' imitations of shrimps that pandered to the fishes' memories of the sea. He said that they could sometimes, with advantage, be lightly leaded to fish deep in heavy water (so the brass tube principle is not new). Younger was one of the many who preferred splices to ferrules. He mentions fellow anglers, including James Baillie (1815–46) as an habitual 'upstreamer' (as also did J G Bertram, mentioned previously).

Conrad Voss Bark, according to his book *A History of Fly Fishing* (1992), seemingly wanted to make Younger a leading progenitor of the nymph fishing methods associated with the name of G E M Skues (1858–1949). In truth, a crowd of Scottish 'upstreamers' were fishing nymphs through most of the nineteenth-century and perhaps earlier; and who cares if Younger did call them 'maggots'?

Besides his well-known book on fishing, Younger left materials for a staggeringly dull autobiography published in 1881. He was a fine angler but an unremarkable writer on anything else, literary pretensions notwithstanding. Perhaps he knew this when he hoped that 'the reader will be lenient when assured that he has got the very best style the writer can possibly afford from thirty shillings worth of scholastic education'. Anyway, he put first things first: 'I could admire the beautiful in landscape as much as my neighbours . . . yet never could find time for the disposition of sentiment while sallying out on a fishing excursion'. (Tom Stoddart had similar sensible views of the beauties of nature.) According to Younger, over-attachment to trivial matters such as landscape led to 'those fishing author's sickly preachments'. John Younger was surely one of the more picturesque figures we have to deal with.

8
Late-nineteenth century

I n this chapter, as in the preceding one, I look at authors whose works do not seem to merit a chapter apiece. As before, I adopt an alphabetical order. The period covered is approximately 1870 on to early this century, because authors writing in the early twentieth century would have been nineteenth-century anglers. Before starting the list it may be useful to record two works designed to help the sporting tourist on his way, namely the guides to travel, accommodation and sport provided by J W Lyall, *The Sportsman's Tourist's and General Timetables* (1877–1915), and Robert Hall, *The Highland Sportsman* (1882, 1884, 1886). Both refer to fishing but neither is of real angling concern. They reflect the growing interest in Scottish sports also found in the *Fishing Gazette* of the day (see Chapter 11). Probably, there were other such books but I have not searched for them.

The first author to be reviewed is Robert Burns Begg. He is a locally specialised writer whose fascinating book on Loch Leven first appeared under the authorship of 'An ex-President of the Kinross-Shire Fishing Club'. The book, *The Loch Leven Angler* (1874), was mostly based on articles from the *Kinross-Shire Advertiser*. The author was said by Ford (1984) to have been a grand-nephew of the poet Robert Burns, himself a 'lad o' pairts' but no angler. Though an ardent local angler, Begg had the right ideas about Loch Leven as a sort of 'Brobdingnagian Fish-pond' that had been a commercial fishery since medieval times but of no sporting consequence until the mid-nineteenth century. An important survey of 1809 preceded major works undertaken by the then proprietor, Graham, to drain land, drop the water level by some feet and give better water control for the mills. Area fell by 19 per cent. The 'New Cut', four miles long, was opened in 1830. Netting throve but the last char ('gellytroch trout') went in 1837. Pike, perch and eels also did well and were taken commercially in vast quantities. Angling developed from about 1850 and the general pattern, familiar today, of 3–4 small flies fished over the front of the boat broadside on to the wind, preferrably in an east wind and a good wave, was soon established. Trout netting was stopped in 1873 and angling ruled thereafter, with very uneven success. At best, there were many pounders (catches generally peaking seasonally in May–June) but the place was never universally loved. Tom Stoddart, among others, spoke ill of it and modern anglers (myself included) tend to regard favourable reports either as freaks or as examples of Stoddart's 'roseate fiction'. Whatever the angling status of Loch Leven, Begg's book is a good one. The water became the scene of the main Scottish competitive angling event and, later, of an annual international competition. The best historical account of catches and competitions is to be found in David Biggart's excellent book *The Scottish National Angling Club Associations, 1880–1980* (1979). The general picture is of wild fluctuations between years and an overall decline in recent decades.

'Black Palmer' on *Scotch Loch Fishing* (1882) seems to have been a Glaswegian and the only author on the list to have preserved his pseudonymity. His is a good, practical book that advocates short casts on downwind drifts, trolling if one must, dark flies on bright days, and only two flies per cast, with smaller sizes preferred. It is an agreeable but unremarkable work.

William Sorley Brown ('Rainbow') published his *Secrets of Border Angling* in 1907 but hardly disclosed any secrets unknown to the authors of 50 years before. However, he did mention the dry fly as a very recent introduction (improbable) to the Borders and wondered why it had been so neglected. His writing does not encourage the belief that he was a really skilled or successful angler.

W L Calderwood was Inspector of Salmon Fisheries for Scotland and a Fellow of the Royal Society of Edinburgh. He was a professional biologist who wrote two substantial books on salmon biology which were published in the 1930s. For the angler, his earlier book is much more important. *The Salmon Rivers and Lochs of Scotland* (1909, 1921) is an important work which goes back to nineteenth-century experience and is well supported by illustrations and maps.

A H Chaytor's book, *Letters to a Salmon Fisher's Sons* (1920, 1919, 1925), is an agreeable and lucid work by a man who clearly fished much for Scottish salmon though where he did so is not clear. His chapter 29 on angling literature should be read with caution because   43 it seems as though he confused John Younger with David Webster. As to the latter (see below) he says that a Doctor Livingstone of Wishaw 'ghosted' his book for him.

Elsewhere, I mention R A Chrystal's thoughtful works in connection with Hamish Stuart (see Chapter 9). On this time-scale he is very late but his experience went well back into the nineteenth-century. He was old enough to have seen 'straps' of flies in use on the Clyde and tells an agreeable anecdote of a gamekeeper who shot off the top of a poacher's rod: 'rough and ready and ready to be rough'. Some contemporary anglers may be especially interested in his liking for deep, slow, wet flies on a sunken line, managed by touch alone, which seems to anticipate current reservoir practice. He thought that the bob fly in Scotland was over-estimated. I do, too.

Charles H Cook, an English angler better known by his pseudonym, 'John Bickerdyke', just gets a place here because he fished in Lewis ('Thule' to him, which he considered to be the end of the earth) in the early 1890s. In his book *Days in Thule with Rod, Gun and Camera* (1894, 1897) he writes agreeably of salmon, trout and sea trout and had a good day, with light tackle, pursuing haddies in the bay.

William Dawson's guidebook *Dawson's Illustrated Guide to the Borderland* (1885) is, according to R J W Coleby (1979), an obscure work that appeared under several long but different titles in the 1890s. I have not seen it and do not propose to try very hard to do so.

Frederick Fernie was the first dry fly fanatic in Scotland or, at least, the first to write a book about it, entitled *Dry Fly Fishing in Border Waters* (1912). It is a very good book though curiously unnoticed by J W Hills (1921). It also went unmentioned by the excellent R C Bridgett (1922, 1929), though he certainly knew of it: my copy bears Bridgett's autographed initials! The floating fly was widely used in England from the 1860s onwards but became popular in Scotland only from the end of the century. If other writers neglected Fernie, however, he too neglected his predecessors and one gets no more than a hint from him that the dry fly (and its 'pure' doctrine) was invented in England rather than in the Borders. As I have remarked elsewhere in this book, angling writers really have been rather bad at reading the literature and citing their predecessors. Fernie, however, wanted, as others have done, to make Stewart 'really' a dry fly fisher (which is silly). But he was a sharp observer and agreed with Hamish Stuart that loch trout tended to be territorial.

Francis Francis (1822–86) was one of the angling immortals who, like Tom Stoddart, lived to fish. He was born in Devonshire and much of his experience was in England. But he travelled widely, fished thoughtfully and wrote well. His great *Book on Angling* (1867–1920) is still well worth reading but has no special Scottish content. His other major work, *By Lake and River* (1874) records travels, that is, four 'rambles' in the north of England and Scotland. The first 'rambles' covered north-eastern England and Tweed; the second, Aberdeen, Inverness, Beauly, Findhorn, Conon, Spey, Tay, and back to Tweed; the third went west to Inveraray, Loch Awe (where he lost a ferox and experienced 'the ethereal mildness of a severe May'), Lochs Leven, Lomond, Arklet, Katrine and Ard; and the fourth went to Thurso and Strathmore Lodge for shooting as well as salmon fishing.

On the Tweed, at various times, he met several local worthies including Wright, Forrest and Kerss; while in Edinburgh he met Stewart and Russel (editor of *The Scotsman* and an angling friend of Tom Stoddart). He was a good general angler who also chased pike, recommended Scottish piking to his Thames friends, liked the pike and perch of Loch Awe and thought that Loch Ard would be much improved by the hiring of 'a regular old Thames netsman'. The work is not without a few *longueurs* but it remains highly readable as one of the best available pictures of the totality of Scottish angling in the 1860s–1870s. Clearly, many more trips than just the four 'rambles' are represented and the sequences of waters defy geographical logic. In this, he is nearly as hard to follow as Thornton. He identified the Stanley water of the Tay as the scene of Mr Briggs's triumph, recorded by John Leech.

Augustus Grimble was an ardently sporting Englishman who lived in Brighton and was sufficiently wealthy to visit the Highlands annually from 1857 onwards. He was more of a shooter than an angler and killed vast numbers of birds, but he was also a serious salmon fisher and worth reading on the subject, even if one does, on occasion, get a bit tired of the slaughter, the country houses, the overfed guests and the name dropping. He wrote several books, the interesting parts condensed into the one handsome reprint entitled *Shooting and Salmon Fishing and Highland Sport* (1902). A few

45

interesting and/or quotable points follow. Poaching was Rampant and Ought to be Stopped; it could be discouraged by the use of 'empty three-dozen champagne cases, filled with stones and porcupined with long, strong nails'. What reader has even seen such a champagne case?

He gave trout a try at Loch Leven and thought the fishings 'well arranged and devoid of cockney surroundings' (what else would a gentleman expect?). One should be wary, he thought, of exaggerated claims for excellence for rivers and hence of high rents. He liked an 18-foot spliced greenheart rod and advocated the Spey cast but his pictures are not very convincing (maybe not his fault). He thought a metal reel was better than a wooden or vulcanite one because, if dented, it could be mended by 'any blacksmith' (yes, he wrote 'blacksmith'). He mostly fished the fly and tied his own but was not averse to artificial spinners and minnows (the latter brought alive by the hundred in England, of course, and carried to Scotland). Grimble was not one of the great angling writers but he had his moments and there were none quite so relentlessly gentlemanly. Gentlemanly or no, however, he did not object to worms, believed in treating a hooked salmon quite roughly and held the minute-per-pound rule.

Edward Hamilton MD FLS was a (presumably) Scottish medic, born in 1815, who fished widely in Scotland from about 1850. He is depicted in the *Fishing Gazette* (1889, 19, p. 155). He spent two months per year from about 1870, mostly in the north-west of Scotland (for example on Spean, Ness, Lochy and Elchaig). He wrote a rather good book, *Recollections of Fly Fishing for Salmon, Trout and Grayling* (1891), about his experiences and correctly interpreted the biology of the salmonids (as I suppose an FLS should do by that time). He suspected, with other diverse authors such as Begg and Francis, that the silvery cast of Loch Leven fish denoted a sea trout ancestry. He knew of the dry fly but preferred the wet, fished upstream (if possible), did not believe much in wind, water, time or weather for trout fishing and preferred a bright fly for a bright day. He did not think highly of local fly preferences and tells an agreeable story of Old Robertson who dismissed Hamilton's fly as 'no good on this water'; after five 'fish', he looked again and said 'I didnae see yon wee bit of blue jay feather; the fish are very fond of that colour'. I am reminded of a friend who showed his fly to a Sutherland ghillie. The old boy said 'I don't wish to contemn your fly, surr, but you'll no be catching fish on that thing here'. He was wrong, alas.

J A Harvie-Brown LLD FZS FRSE (1844–1916) (sometimes Harvey Brown) was a devoted 'upstreamer' and Stewart follower in most respects, and a supporter of the short split-cane rod and tapered silk line. His book, *The Wonderful Trout* (1898), is a good and thoughtful one, as befits a professional zoologist and FRSE. He calculated, for instance, that the upstreamer might make 15 casts per minute or 4,000–5,000 per day: 'hard pounding this, gentlemen' with a big cane rod! On 'coming short', he offered an interesting suggestion that trout were not, as is usually thought, mouthing the fly but flicking it (contemptuously?) with their tails on turning away. One might expect a great many trout thus to be foul-hooked but they are not. Harvie-Brown's idea, though, is supported by the simple experiment of trying to foul-hook a dead fish; even sharp hooks are easily shown to bounce off trout scales, which are very tough objects. Try it and see! He advocated the Stewartian short line (always upstream of course) and was a bit coy in writing about the use of baits.

Davies Hodge ('Yellow Body') was a Dundee journalist who died in 1889 (*Fishing Gazette*, 1889, 18, p. 33), having fished for many years and written a rather good book entitled *Angling Days on Scotch Lochs* (1884). His chapters are mostly reprinted sketches from the *Dundee Advertiser* and he directs the reader to 'Black Palmer' (see above) for practical advice. He fished widely, from Loch Ba near Dalmally (scores of tiddlers) to Lochs Clunie, Griam and Shin in the north and, nearer home, Loch Leven. On the last ('a most fickle loch') his club had a fairish day in 1873 but he seems to have loved the place as little as many other anglers. It is not quite clear why, but he and his companions may have christened the 'Zulu' fly.

William Earl Hodgson was an ardent angler who lived for many years in Aberfeldy, though it may be difficult to discern any Scottish content in much of his writing. He wrote four rather sensible but uninspiring books of which three need not concern us here. His *Salmon Fishing* (1906), however, has a very substantial Scottish content and particular interest centres on his Chapter 6, 'Are the Salmon Declining?'. Not content with selected local hearsay, as most writers have been, even to the present day, he enquired systematically throughout the UK and recorded local opinions fully. I scored his 47 results on a scale from –2 (disastrous), through –1, 0, +1 to +2 (excellent) and found the following (frequencies of waters):

Score	–2	–1	0	+1	+2
Scotland	4	10	32	6	2
Ireland	5	19	10	1	0
England & Wales	3	7	12	5	2

Allied to the observation that independent remarks about one water sometimes conflicted, these results do not suggest any widespread support for the belief that 'the salmon is not long to be in the land'. It is still in terminal decline nearly a century later, though the belief may have better justification now than then. Anyway, Hodgson was a level-headed and empirical sceptic: valuable men, sceptics!

George Kelson was the 'father' of the salmon fly in its heyday during the 1890s and wrote a splendid book about it entitled *The Salmon Fly* (1895); it is beautifully illustrated and gives details on tying. He was clearly a very practical salmon angler, though a poor writer, and this book shares some excellent line drawings with his later work, *Tips* (1901). Kelson was English but had clearly fished much in Scotland; he must have been a professional or something near it because he was a relentless advertiser for his own (and some other people's) products. The *Fishing Gazette* (1884–5, 8–11) has a series of confused but well illustrated articles by him. Much later, the same magazine (1896, 32) carried a rather brutal review of his book, accusing him, not unjustly, of plagiarism and self-advertisement. A nasty review in the generally bland *Fishing Gazette* is noteworthy and the reviewer really did have his knife out.

A contemporary addition to the Kelson literature is the book *The Land and Water Salmon Flies, 1886–1902* (1994), based on published articles collected by the editor for the Fly Fishers' Classic Library. It is stated that it gives authoritative dressings and many fine coloured plates.

Arthur E Knox MA FLS was a general naturalist as well as an ardent Spey Salmon fisher. He had his duckings and adventures and in his book on that great river, *Autumns on the Spey* (1872) provides what is probably the best list of authentic 'old Spey flies' of the day, mostly sombre mallard patterns, with heron hackles.

Henry Lamond was a Glasgow lawyer (born 1869) whose angling experience went well back into the nineteenth-century. His six books, however, are hardly weighty enough to deserve extensive treatment here, good as they are in parts. The first four (1911, 1914, 1921a, 1921b) are mostly reprinted, rather blethery articles from the *Glasgow Herald*. They do, however, contain an authentic refutation of 'The Great Salmon Myth', which stated that apprentices or indentured workers might not, by Scottish Law, be fed salmon more than so many times per week. Franck and Walter Scott, said Lamond, were both at least partly responsible for a piece of what he regarded as legal nonsense, a myth as silly as the later one about Russian soldiers with snow on their boots.

His last two books are much more substantial. *Loch Lomond* (1931) is a fascinating history of Loch Lomond angling from Franck and Thornton onwards. He knew anyone who was anyone, including Hamish Stuart who had 'an easy volubility which never faltered' and was responsible for 'glaring fallacies'. His final book, *Days and Ways* (1932), is a very readable summary of a lifetime's fishing experience, in lochs and rivers, for salmon, ferox, pike and perch in freshwater, and for 'coalies' in the sea. He had little regard for Loch Leven except as a place for competitions. He promoted angling associations and sensible legislation to protect angling interests. On tackle, he remarked that split cane was rare in Scotland until 1890–1900 and that the English dry fly vogue had had little effect, though it had been popular on the Tweed since 1910 and R C Bridgett (see Chapter 10) had promoted it.

Andrew Lang's *Angling Sketches* (1891, 1895) are little more than agreeable chit-chat but he had fished widely, from youth in the Borders, later in the North, which gave rise to an anecdote about a monstrous four-pounder among the four-ouncers of Loch Borralan. He disliked Loch Leven ('crowded and cockneyfied by competitions') and thought 'trolling a minnow from a boat in Loch Leven probably the lowest form of angling'.

Leitch's book, *A Scottish Fly Fisher* (1911) is an agreeable work with many sensible observations, though its 'purpose is not instructive'. He did not favour entomology, preferred fishing to scenery (what angler did not, starting with Stoddart and Younger?), thought Loch Leven 'tainted with commercialism', regarded seasonal choice of fly as absurd and ghillies as often wrong, was anti-dry-fly, was an 49 'upstreamer' if possible and liked to row upwind when fishing the loch. Unremarkable but ever sensible.

Alexander Mackie, author of *The Art of Worm Fishing* (1912), was an Aberdonian and a devoted clear-water, upstream wormer. He followed Stewart in all essentials but thought that a 'treatise' rather than a mere chapter was needed; it is not, in my opinion, evident that he was right but his book is a good one. Even in those days, worms could be bought and he preferred the 'blue nose' to the 'brandling'. He liked to fish early or late in the day, wading quietly or creeping upstream. At the right time, trout were everywhere and to catch parr was a bad sign.

James McNee of Pitlochry was a professional fisher who wrote an excellent series of articles entitled 'Trout Angling' in the *Fishing Gazette* of 1885 and thus deserves a place in the bibliography. He reckoned that he had caught 'hundreds' of three-pounders in the Tay, and fished upstream with two or three small flies thrown at rising fish. If there were no rises, he said, then fish with bait – simple! Three-pounders are assured.

John MacVine was born in 1820 and was 70 when he published his very readable book, *Sixty-three Years Angling*, in 1891. Though he lived much of his life as an English businessman, he fished often in Scotland from boyhood onwards, met several Tweed notables of the 1850s such as Stewart and Russel, fished Dee and Don and finally retired to live again in Scotland, near Peebles in 1882 and later at Perth. He was very conceited regarding his own abilities and had decided views on all angling matters. For example, he boasted of his own casting skills, said that locals on the Don rushed to their rods when he appeared and wrote the splendid sentence: 'The same perseverance, energy and assiduity which characterised the author's success in angling, when applied to business affairs, were productive of similar results.' He even took customers fishing and persuaded them to order goods 'far in excess of their actual requirements'. He also refers to his well-known 'intrepid daring in wading'. But what is a bit of conceit from an excellent angler and a more than usually readable writer (even though he did pen some lamentable verses, too).

He thought that Loch Tay trolling 'cannot be called either angling or pleasure', was contemptuous of harling as 'unscientific', disliked Loch Leven (but merely called it 'an uncertain lake'). Less justifiably, he attributed salmon disease to dirt, artificial manures, pollution, sheep dip and land drainage; grouse and potatoes were similarly afflicted, he said. Although his verse was generally bad, there is worse elsewhere, and one piece strikes a chord: a longish poem entitled *An Honest Angler's Ode on Tweed*. It is the only piece of verse I know in which pollution and poaching vie with the purple patches; the evils were and are real enough but would have been better described in plain prose.

Peter D Malloch wrote excellent articles on Tay trouting in the *Fishing Gazette* during the 1880s. He was a renowned Perth tackle dealer, justly famous for his salmon flies, and a considerable authority on the biology of the salmonids. He did not write any angling books but his *Fishing Gazette* articles of 1890 are published under the title *Salmon Flies and How to Make Them* by the Fly Fishers' Classic Library (1994). It is related in Chapter 11 how Malloch was the most successful Scottish national competitor in history and his remarkable achievements are unlikely ever to be equalled.

Sir Herbert Maxwell was very important as a public figure devoted to the cause of Scottish angling, to fisheries management and to angling literature. But his book, *Salmon and Sea Trout* (1898), is rather dull and perfunctory, being nearly all conventional material about salmon on the fly.

George Rooper's book entitled *Thames and Tweed* (1870, 1876, 1894) seems to be good on the Thames, not so good on the Tweed, though he certainly fished in Scotland and Ireland. He is interesting on the tackle of the day and remarked that 'no fisherman ever goes out without a good knife, a piece of string, a corkscrew and a button hook in his pocket'. A button hook?

Tom Speedy's *The Natural History of Sport in Scotland* (1920) is almost a reprint of his 1884 book. Speedy was born in 1846 and, like his father, was in estate employ. His writings were mostly about shooting but he was a good naturalist and an experienced angler. As a keeper, he needed to produce fish to order and clearly did so. But he was neither an innovator nor an interesting writer.

Dr Thomas Fair Hetherington Spence, R P Wilson and A N Other were the 'Three Anglers' who wrote the excellent and sternly practical book *How to Catch Trout* (1888, 1908). Thanks to Mr R J W Coleby, it is known that the first two authors were Edinburghians. T F H Spence was a distinguished medic, a surgeon who

51

qualified in the University in 1875; R P Wilson often appears in the *Scots Angler* (see Chapter 11); the third may have been either Lewis Spence or Dr William Badger, another Edinburgh medic who qualified in 1878 and worked mostly in public health (as MOH, Penicuik, for example). The Medical Register shows that Spence and Badger were still in practice in 1900.

The book is a densely written, authoritative and comprehensive account of Scottish trout fishing in the late nineteenth-century. The authors were 'upstreamers' in principle but were prepared to adapt practice to circumstance. They mostly fished light, Tweed-style flies but were accustomed to fish a dry fly in the flats. They also used worm, creeper, mayfly or minnow when appropriate (and favoured giving the worm a little motion in still water). They considered loch fishing to be 'an agreeable pastime' but not very skilful, though they were obviously good at it and favoured the ploy of side-casting from a boat rowed slowly upwind. They were not very keen on trolling but were prepared to try it and also prepared to throw large worms, sink and draw, into burn-mouths. By the time of their last edition, the long-awaited Freshwater Fish (Scotland) Act had been passed and there was a close-time, 15 October to 28 February. This is a really excellent book as a crisp and readable summary of established practice and it is hard to see how it could, within its chosen limits, be bettered.

John Stirling was a staunch traditionalist who started fishing in 1876. His first work, *Andrew Smith. To his Memory* (1907), was an edition of the essays of Andrew Smith. Smith (1874–1905) was an Edinburgh Writer to the Signet, editor of the short-lived *Scots Angler* (see Chapter 11) and a notable fighter for close-time under law (which was achieved in 1902). He died, prematurely, of typhoid, and John Stirling's work is a generous tribute to an admirable man. Stirling's one big book, *Fifty Years with the Rod* (1929), starts with a good account of the close-time Act of 1902 but is otherwise staunchly traditional. He stayed with the long rod nearly all his life, but allowed a shorter weapon for the dry fly. His practical how-to-do-it chapters are followed by a long section entitled 'Angling Haunts', anecdotes spread over much of Scotland. They carry conviction because, as he said, 'my fishing diaries are punctuated with disasters'. I especially liked his account of outings to Loch Lyon (pp. 170–72), fearsome walks starting in 1881. His last book, *Fishing for Trout and Sea Trout* (1931), was quite explicitly a condensation of the practical parts of the preceding book and is of little interest.

John Tait, clearly a Shetlander, must be considered as the anonymous author of *Angler's Guide for the Shetlands* (1903, published by John Tait and Co., Lerwick). He sold fishing tackle and his book is an excellent, practical and rather well-written work. He favoured quite big greenheart rods and any fly, bait or lure that would do for trout and sea trout in burn, loch or voe. He perhaps gives more emphasis to dapping natural flies on a light line than was usual at the time. But, neither here nor anywhere else as early as this, have I found mention of a floss dapping line. However, the Shetlands are very windy indeed and the line would often hardly matter; after all, many a fisher in the North has seen a salmon line streaming out nearly horizontally.

Ewen M Tod was son of General Tod of Morningside, Edinburgh. He lived in Queensland for a time and later practised dentistry in Brighton (*Fishing Gazette*, 1886, 13, p. 362). Whatever his professional life-style, he also practised the art of angling in Scotland from about 1860 and wrote a good but somewhat turgid book, *Wet Fly Fishing Methodically Treated* (1903), about fly fishing in streams there. From this book, one would hardly notice that lochs existed but his FG articles (see below) tell us otherwise. He did not have much use for the dry fly in Scotland but fished with bait and spinners, as revealed in a stream of articles in the *Fishing Gazette* (1887–1900). He was clearly something of an inventor of gadgets such as 'wee doubles'. Eyed flies were then becoming the norm. Tod also has some pungent remarks about the chaotic size scales adopted by makers (alas, no better now than they were then). He was a convinced Stewartian 'upstreamer' and liked 'wee' flies and split cane, but disliked flashy varnish. Tod, then, was an expert traditionalist with inventive habits and something of a specialist on small waters. His *Fishing Gazette* articles cover a somewhat wider field than his book, including an excellent polemic (1891, 22, p. 380) on the 'puffing' of reports by ghillies in response to covert bribes by hoteliers; neither were the 'chentlemen', in his opinion, always all that truthful about their catches. He also departed from received wisdom on the loch by enjoying fishing from the shore and in deliberately choosing to fish into wind, foam and debris on the windward shore (*Fishing Gazette*, 1889, 35, p. 162). This practice is still much recommended but not so much practised.

53

David Webster was, in my opinion, nearly one of the immortals. He was a professional fisher, a traditional Tweed–Clyde trouter, though he acknowledged the existence of salmon, sea trout, pike and (oh horror!) grayling. The last, he thought, was popular with English anglers because it was 'easily deceived and easily caught'; the trout was a far superior fish and better eating, too. Webster used a long, spliced rod (13.5 feet) with a loop spliced to the tip, a tapered horsehair line of 18–20 feet, 8–10 flies on a 16-foot gut leader, with the terminal gear constituting the 'strap', as seen occasionally up to quite recent times. He managed all this, not by Stewart-style overhead casting (who would dare?), but by a sort of aerial roll or switch which, he reckoned, gave him accuracy, even upwind, at 40–50 feet (quite far enough for a cautious 'upstreamer'). He was, indeed, a convinced 'upstreamer' (with Younger and 15 years before Stewart, he said) and believed in imitative patterns which were never to be 'worked'. On Clyde in due season each year, he even took the Green Drake seriously, called locally the 'Yellow Fly'; is it there still? Naturally, baits and minnows also had their place in his repertoire. He believed in a large creel and reckoned to take 10–15 pounds of fish per day, even though 'fishing had greatly declined in these altered and degenerate times' and 'over-fished, impoverished and polluted streams'. What would he say nowadays?

So Webster was a fanatical and successful fisher, a traditionalist with a difference. He probably had little or no education and Chaytor (see page 43) says that his book, *The Angler and the Loop-Rod* (1885), was 'ghosted' by a Dr Livingstone of Wishaw. There was a Robert Livingstone (MD, Glasgow, 1847) who practised in Wishaw about the right time, so what Chaytor says may well be true, but seems to be uncorroborated. If so, Dr Livingstone wrote well but was rather too fond of purple patches. My enthusiasm for Webster was not shared by an anonymous reviewer in the *Fishing Gazette* (1885, 11, p.106). He niggled at Webster's old-fashioned habits and his gibes at other writers (not unfairly) but one cannot avoid the impression that what really upset the reviewer was the remark about grayling being favoured by English anglers because they were stupid and easy to catch (the fish, not the anglers).

Finally, Archibald Young's book, *Angler's and Sketcher's Guide to Sutherland* (1880), is agreeable but not very weighty. It is mostly reprinted from *Scotsman* articles. Young was an Edinburghian, an advocate and Commissioner of Scotch Salmon Fisheries. He did a six-week tour from Lairg, going clockwise, northwards and then down the west coast. He had excellent baskets on the Loyal–Craggie–Slaim Lochs, including some fine ferox, and also did well around Assynt. Curiously, he said that the Durness lochs were reckoned to be good but mentions neither the limestone nor their extraordinary clarity, so probably did not fish them. In this he was unremarkable because I don't recall a single nineteenth-century author who realised just how remarkable those limestone waters are. No doubt the locals knew but had the good sense not to tell the Sassenachs. But it is possible that the predominant fish populations were still char rather than trout and the latter awaited an effective stocking policy by the landlords and hoteliers. Sea trout, common in the area, may have been involved and the silvery glitter of fish from Croispol has often been remarked upon. The biggest brown trout I ever caught was a gorgeous silvery beast from Croispol taken in a glaring, sunny calm. Surprises come rarely in those lochs but, when they do, they are spectacular.

9
Hamish Stuart

S tuart was a journalist who worked for many years in Scarborough, fished from the 1860s onwards, died of TB at sea in 1914 and wrote one important book, *Lochs and Loch Fishing* (1899). This work is long, ill-constructed, windy and over-fluently written, as befits a journalist. Stuart himself said it was 'the hasty product of thirty evenings' work after days of such toil as modern "evening paper" journalism necessitates'. I calculate that he must have written about 5,600 words per night to fill 390 pages at such speed. The book contains a lot of good and interesting information but is loaded with windy blether, some of it barely intelligible, which may be why few later writers seem to have praised or even tried to read it; a shorter book of only a third or less in length, would have been far better. He also left a draft of *The Book of Sea Trout*, edited for publication by the novelist Rafael Sabatini (1917, 1952). As a prolific journalist, Stewart must have written articles but I have seen only a few little pieces in the *Fishing Gazette*.

At all events, he would have been quite forgotten but for his *Lochs and Loch Fishing*. Discounting the blether, he was clearly a very competent and successful angler of vast experience who had pursued brown trout, sea trout and salmon in hundreds (he said more than 200) of Scottish lochs, especially in the west and the Hebrides. He was knowledgeable and observant on fish biology and was convinced that loch trout tend to have 'lies'. Indeed, he regarded a loch as 'a large pool in a currentless river' and concluded (surely mistakenly and by an impenetrable logic) that, therefore, the dry fly was useless. He thought that loch fishing was difficult and that success went only to the expert (like Hamish Stuart, for example, who caught three or four times as many fish as other anglers). As to flies, he held that a hint of imitation was sensible but derided entomology; a shrimp on the tail, a beetle in the middle and an ephemerid on the bob would serve, so a teal-and-red, a heckham-peckham and anything fuzzy were basic (which did not stop him listing dozens of patterns). His disdain for entomology (remember that this was post-Halford) was expressed in his remark that exact imitation: 'has bred a race of prejudiced, exclusive and pedantic entomologists, among whom may be found not a few examples of the angling hypocrite and the angling

pharisee'. That remark must have endeared him to a few True Believers in the South!

He liked small flies whatever the place or the fish and agreed with Franck in preferring a dark fly for a bright day. He insisted on fishing alone, seated in the stern of the boat, with a skilled ghillie to keep the boat and a single-handed rod, such as his Hardy Hotspur of 11 feet. He was against the 'mighty two-handed weapons of the past' (though most of us today would be inclined to take two hands to 11 feet of split cane – I know I would).

He is the only nineteenth-century Scottish angler that I know of to mention the rainbow trout (then just becoming used) and the only one to mention canals where, he conceded, the dry fly might just possibly have a place. He did not explain why the dry fly might work in a canal but not on the loch.

As he said, obviously correctly, surface flies tended to sail downwind whereas sub-surface insects might go anywhere; he therefore insisted on nearly always fishing upwind and it is not clear to me just how the boat was kept to his liking. In principle, at least, the method must have encouraged the two lower flies to have fished deeply and the bob to drift downwind, as he preferred. Contrary to most Scottish loch anglers, then and now, he liked a bright calm, which was to be fished with small flies and, more particularly, with fine gut; he was once rewarded, he said, with three trout of over 18 pounds in 39 minutes on size 13 hooks (though who knows how big they were?). Nowhere in his book, I think, is there any hint that he practised or tolerated the established Scottish custom, habitual then and now, of fishing a short line over the front of a freely drifting boat.

Stuart disapproved of trolling on a somewhat ambiguous sporting principle: 'Now as the aim of scientific angling is to reconcile expediency with morality, policy with honesty and, in a word, to cultivate a moral utilitarianism, I may here interpolate a few observations on a method of using the minnow –'. The inventor of 'Malloch's ingenious loch troller . . . must have felt many a pang of conscientious regret'. I bet Peter Malloch felt no such pangs and Stuart's conscience was elastic enough to allow him to do a bit of spinning, which was not only more moral than trolling but also more effective. Elsewhere, he admits that to throw flies sideways from a rowed boat can be effective, a tactic which must surely be verging on some moral boundary.

Generally, I found Hamish Stuart's book thoughtful and rewarding but difficult to read carefully enough to extract the sense from the windy drivel. Nowadays, it would be very hard to apply his principles in any detail because where does one even find boats with ghillies on good lochs, let alone afford them. Anyway, the fish probably are not there and, indeed, were already in decline in Stuart's day.

The only thoughtful and sympathetic commentary on the book that I have seen is that of R A Chrystal, *Angling Theories and Methods* (1927), who also clearly had some difficulty in understanding Stuart's opaque prose and, in particular, how he managed the boat. I hope that this chapter and Chrystal's advocacy will encourage other anglers to read and think about Hamish Stuart's ideas, whatever the literary obstacles. Some writers, such as Lamond (1931, see Chapter 8) could not stand him but there really is something there, underneath the blether.

10
Robert Currie Bridgett

obert Currie Bridgett (1880–1961) was the last of the important Scottish angling writers on my list. He was prolific (five books and innumerable articles in the *Glasgow Herald*, which I have not tried to track down), but so late that there must be some doubt as to whether he should have been included at all. His books were all written in the 1920s but his experience must have started near the end of the nineteenth-century. However, he wrote good material, and the decision was mine to include him.

There is little biographical information available. From the evidence of his books, he lived near Glasgow, wrote pieces for the *Glasgow Herald* but, despite his distinction, attracted only a short obituary notice on his death in retirement at Abington in 1961. His omission from the DNB is, like that of Stewart, ridiculous. For many years he was a school teacher (holding an MA and BSc) and he finally held the post of Rector of Lanark Grammar School. Scraps of evidence suggest that he was a scientist/mathematician. Indeed, Richard Hunter has shown me a small pedagogical work demonstrating that Bridgett taught science.

His writings were lucid and well composed but just a little verbose (in the Dominie tradition, perhaps?). He is excellent in tight, closely argued instructional passages, where his experience, good sense and lucidity are apparent. He is not so good on anecdote where (hardly surprisingly, considering the sheer volume of his writings) the same tales (or at least seemingly, the same tales) tend to recur. He must have kept very detailed notes or diaries or had a remarkable capacity for recall. But even the anecdotes are not mere tales oft retold but generally convey good, practical angling points from a very experienced fisherman.

His five books are (he was admirably but unusually economical of words in his titles): *Dry Fly Fishing* (1922, 1929); *By Loch and Stream. Angling Sketches* (1922, 1928); *Loch Fishing in Theory and Practice* (1924, 1926, 1962); *Tight Lines. Angling Sketches* (1926);

Sea Trout Fishing (1929). Of these, the first, third and fifth are essentially excellent how-to-do-it books in the first half of each, followed by anecdotal chapters about specific places. The second and fourth are entirely anecdotal and explicitly owe much to the *Glasgow Herald*; but, being Bridgett anecdotes, the books are none the worse for that, for there are many good observations.

As an angler, Bridgett was first and foremost a trouter, though he also sought sea trout and, to a lesser extent and apparently later in life, salmon. He was very successful and had many catches that, to us today, appear huge but, to Bridgett, reflected the decline in Scottish trouting since Stewart. Nevertheless, a dozen or two half-pounders seem sufficiently remarkable to me. On the other hand, he does not appear to record the capture of monsters. He angled widely, mostly in southern and central Scotland, in lochs, rivers, waters and burns. He reckoned to have fished over 100 lochs (*cf* Hamish Stuart's claim for over 200, see Chapter 9). Though clearly very successful, Bridgett had his blanks (six in a row at one reservoir near Glasgow, he wrote) but one suspects that they were few because he was an excellent angler fishing at a time when there were still plenty of wild trout. He had kind, indeed often enthusiastic, things to say about many places he fished but had the usual qualifications as to Loch Leven: 'Despite bad seasons, poor sport, weary days and unpleasant evenings, Loch Leven contrives to retain its old fascination for us' (*Tight Lines*, 1926). One wonders why he bothered.

Bridgett was essentially a fly fisher for whom the occasional use of worm, creeper or minnow might be justified; but he loathed trolling and disapproved of dapping on the grounds that in one place it was too easy and in another, in a heavy wind, 'dapping is forced upon the angler, not selected'. I recall no mention of floss lines in his writings but he was clearly quite good at 'dibbling' in an overgrown stream.

He liked long, fine leaders and advised two or three flies rather than the customary four. He even used (I think originally) pairs of contrasted floaters. He fished wet or dry and tried to match the trout food of the moment, whether shrimp, nymph, hatcher or adult, sedge, beetle, ephemerid or whatever. But he was not theological about patterns and was quite prepared to accept unusual identities for successful ones; thus the March Brown artificial was usually a shrimp (Hamish Stuart identified the Teal-and-Red as a shrimp!) and he greatly favoured the split-wing Butcher on the bob, for no particular reason except that it worked. He was the first writer that I know of to spot the importance of midge larvae in the trout's diet but did not explicitly try to imitate them, beyond insisting on the value of a green body on a sunk fly (for example, a Teal-and-Green). Whether on loch or river, Bridgett tended to use a floater if trout were moving and to go deep if they were not, but to search extensively with either. On the river, he even indulged quite explicitly in what became called, decades later, the 'induced take': 'the lure can be made to rise and fall in the water' (*Tight Lines*, 1926).

In principle, he did not believe in 'fisherman's weather' as anything other than weather in which fishermen caught fish: the fish decided, so ignore the weather and fish on. The only clear principle was that, on the river, the breeze had to be upstream: if it was not, move on or go home. Elsewhere, he was less decided and the usual grey skies and mild westerly breezes were held to be attractive.

On the river, needless to say, he was a convinced Stewartian 'upstreamer', both dry and wet. He even argued that Stewart himself (because he recognised how critical was the moment of landing the flies) was 'really' a dry fly fisher, except that his dry flies were wet and he fished too many of them. Odd logic indeed but it recurs in the literature and has appeared in preceding chapters in this book. Generally, one has the impression that Bridgett had read Stewart but no other author: Hamish Stuart might never have fished his 200 lochs nor Fernie written his excellent book 15 years before (a work which Bridgett certainly knew existed). As to the dry fly, not only did Bridgett manage to ignore Fernie, carelessly or wilfully, but he also managed to miss the fact that the English had had a hand in its invention.

I mentioned earlier that Bridgett was just a little verbose. Happily, he was not given to purple patches on the Beauties of Nature but he could and did churn out a lot of high-class, Victorian-style fishing prose. He also wrote much pseudo-Burns in *Tight Lines* and better verses they are, too, than those of most other, more pretentious, angling versifiers. Speech makers at club dinners might do better to look to Bridgett than to Stoddart or to (oh horror!) 'William o' ye West'. In his prose, I particularly like the fact (though it palls after many repetitions) that fishing reels sing, shriek, screech or scream; the lucky trout fisher has occasionally heard such a thing but just a rattle of mild clicks are surely far commoner, are they not? On Loch 61

Lyon, while hauling in a huge basket of one-third-pounders, 'reels were screeching merrily'. I know he liked fine gut but he also recommended firm playing. Since when did tiddlers rush around the loch tearing off line from a competent angler? This point and maybe a few others might suggest minor defects in the accuracy of Bridgett's diary or memory. But, broadly, he appears to be a thoughtful and accurate writer as well as an outstandingly competent angler. He certainly has a place among the Scottish angling immortals and a higher one than most others. It may not have much to do with his skill but he once qualified (1919) as a runner-up in the 'national' competition on Loch Leven (Biggart, 1979).

11
Periodicals

There are only two periodicals worth noting here that have any serious Scottish content. I must confess though to an uneasy feeling that there may have been relevant (but unseen) articles in, for example, the many volumes of *The Field* and *Blackwood's* that I have not even scanned. Pennell's short-lived venture (the *Fisherman's Magazine*, 1 1864) ran to but a single volume, has no real Scottish interest and I ignore it. However, parts of it were incorporated into his *Fishing Gossip* (1866), which is of marginal interest (see Chapter 6 on Stewart).

Of the two periodicals worthy of serious attention, *The Scots Angler, a Monthly Magazine of River and Loch*, did not last long enough to achieve any substantial place, while the *Fishing Gazette*, of blessed memory, is the richest mine of British angling information in existence. It started in 1878 and throve for 88 years; right to the end in 1966, it was a weekly that retained wide interests and the agreeably old-fashioned look of yesteryear. From volume 8, 1884, it ran to two volumes a year, each latterly of about 500–600 pages. I scanned it, with the aid of fairly full, but idiosyncratically constructed, indexes, to volume 41, 1900. At that point, I felt that diminishing returns on my labour had set in so I stopped, aware that there must have been more articles of Scottish interest thereafter. Some day, perhaps, someone will take the FG seriously and develop a comprehensive database – a fearsome labour but the only way to order the inchoate mass of information. My own attempts, I am well aware, are too amateur. Even so, I scanned the indexes to about 20,000 pages of text and hope I made some sense of the Scottish content in the later years of the nineteenth-century.

Of the *Scots Angler*, issued for only a year, there is not a great deal to say. It was edited by an energetic Edinburgh lawyer, Andrew Smith (1874–1905) who, alas, died young of typhoid in addition to overwork, as related by his friend John Stirling (1907, see Chapter 8). Its objects were essentially practical: how and where to fish; and how to promote Scottish angling and protect it from poaching, pollution and mismanagement. This second theme had emerged from time to time, but hardly coherently, over the previous few decades. The *Scots Angler* took it seriously and the magazine's principal achievement was surely to have helped push through the much needed 'Close-time Act' of 1902, a beginning, at least. The last issue of the magazine had a photograph of the close-time petition, 20 yards long, with 10,300 signatures. The best available account of the history and politics of this legislation is by John Stirling (1929, chapter 1).

The writings on practical fishing were mostly about trout but salmon made an appearance and so did perch. Apart from the where-to-fish, anecdotal and humorous contributions (the last whimsical rather than funny, alas) there were many how-to-do-it pieces, often under 'weel-kent' names: Peter Malloch, Tom Spence, R P Wilson, John Stirling, Ewen Tod, the Editor – all sensible, solid writers. Tom Spence was, with reasonable certainty, the Dr Thomas Fair Hetherington Spence of the Three Anglers (see Chapter 8). But anons, initials and pseudonyms abounded, the last including 'Guy Otterstane' (Andrew Smith), 'Orange Partridge', 'Pheasant Tail' and 'Torduff'.

Though there were plenty of angling clubs at the time, the *Scots Angler* was affiliated to none and the sentiment emerged in notes and correspondence that clubs merely existed to hold dinners and competitions (not an unfair view) rather than to promote and protect angling. Some members actively disliked competitions (as many do today) and gave the impression of being friendly fishers but not clubbable ones. This did not stop a number of contributors to the magazine from winning the 'national' or being runners-up on Loch Leven over its first 30 years or so; Peter Malloch was out-standing, of course (Biggart, 1979, pp. 74–5).

The *Fishing Gazette* was predominantly English in content and authorship but, even so, Scottish matters were prominent from the start because there was much excellent game fishing well described in a rich literature and the railways had made many remote Highland parts accessible by the 1870s. Wealthy English sportsmen were therefore quite accustomed to sporting holidays, pursuing deer, grouse, salmon and trout in the northern parts of the British Isles. And had not the Dear Queen herself done much to enliven the holiday, if not the sporting, image of the country?

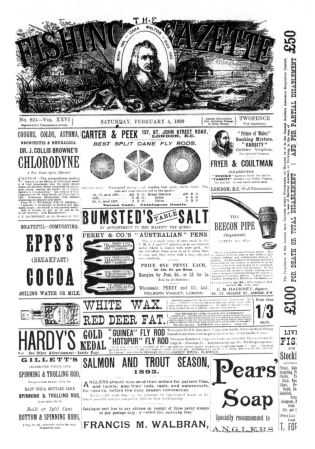

It would be easy to run on too long about the fascinations of the FG. I shall, of necessity, confine myself to rather superficial comments under five convenient headings: promotional pieces, series of how-to-do-it articles, book reviews, personal commentaries and fishing tackle.

First, the promotional pieces. These are very numerous and most volumes contain substantial articles extolling the virtues of some part of Scotland, from the Borders to Shetland and from the Outer Isles to Aberdeenshire. Many particular waters were especially praised (quite rightly too, sometimes), for example the Inchnadamph and Altnacealgach lochs. Travel and accommodation attracted reference and one wonders how often the facts, both touristic and angling, were bent just a little to make the innkeepers and lairdies happy. At all events, enthusiasm reigned and was supported by many pictures

65

(some of them rather good) and mercifully few verses (for example an unquotable disaster on Loch Leven in 1895). In the 1890s, a definite section on 'Scotch Notes' turned up, curiously reminiscent of what may still sometimes be read today: 'Major J F G Barrington-Spilsby and party had 11 nice fish last week and returned many kelts', signed 'Allt-na-Breachlaich, Kildrummie'. The ultimate in promotions for local waters was achieved by about 100 excerpts from the writings of J Watson Lyall (see Chapter 8) during the 1890s. One is left with the impression of much good fishing, a great deal of puffing, a useful service to readers and a few glimpses of sharp common sense. The last is exemplified by AH's remarks (1891, 22, p. 226), regarding Caithness, that to let fishings as mere adjuncts to shootings was bad practice because the fishings were neglected and would have been far better attached to hotels interested in the contentment of their guests: yes!

Second, there were several substantial series of Scottish articles. Those which I consider to be the best were by James McNee (1885), William Murdoch (1886–95), Peter Malloch (1886–95) and Ewen M Tod (1887–1900 and no doubt later). Of these authors, all wrote with authority: McNee was far crisper than the blethery Murdoch (who just could not stop); Malloch's articles are valuable because he never wrote a book about fishing as such but was a superlative angler; and Tod always wrote good sense, even if he did condense most of it into his book (1903, see Chapter 8). McNee (of Pitlochry) is also particularly interesting on DIY matters, tackle management, the substitution of a net by a small folding gaff on the grounds that small trout were best handled but large ones (he had caught hundreds of three-pounders!) were safer gaffed. In addition, there were dull pieces in 1898–1900 ornamented only by the splendid pseudonym 'Blackbeetle'. There were also extensive and very dull quotations from 'Palmer Hackle' (that is, Robert Blakey) on angling tourism and several messy excerpts from Scrope's great book in 1896. Finally, and not least, the indomitable George Kelson promoted George Kelson in a series (1884–85) on salmon casting, fishing and flies. These articles are distinguished by rather good pictures (Kelson is the only angler I can recall who preferred a bowler hat) but terribly confused prose. I suppose, but have not checked, that these articles were expanded into his books of 1895 and 1901.

Third, the reviews of books were many and mostly quite bland: 'Black Palmer', George F Braithwaite, Duncan Fraser, Tom Stoddart (third edition of *Angler's Companion*), George Rooper, 'John Bickerdyke', and William Senior's edition of 'Palmer Hackle's' book were all treated thus. Much more interesting are a substantial essay-review (in 1885) of Clarke's *Angler's Desideratum* (1839) and a rough treatment of Webster's *The Angler and the Loop Rod* (1885). The reviewer here was rattled by Webster's gibes at sundry authors, some English, some Scottish, by his adherence to traditional Clyde tackle and by his dislike of grayling. The reviewer here must be right to imagine the horrors of trying to net a trout attached to a nine-fly 'strap' (Webster did no such thing, of course) but he failed to notice that Webster was a fantastically successful and thoughtful angler and a sort of village genius. I rather hope that R B Marston, generally a reasonable man, did not write this imperceptive review.

There were also several reviews of new works in the period 1896–1900. Thus Kelson's (1895) garbled self-advertisement was quite roughly handled in 1896; the 1898 William Senior edition of Blakey's book and Harvie-Brown's *Wonderful Trout* (1898) received essentially favourable reviews in 1898 (though one reviewer wondered whether W C Stewart had not been just a little over-valued); Ewen M Tod wrote an excellent piece on the new edition of Halford's *Dry Fly Fishing*, pointing out, as Francis Francis also had, long before, that sensible anglers liked and used any fly that worked, dogma notwithstanding. Hamish Stuart's book received an anonymous review that said much the same as I have written here (Chapter 9). The reviewer recognised Stuart's thoughtful experience and good sense but deplored his verbosity (comparing him with Franck!), his too-ready dismissal of the dry fly and his anti-English sneers (the dry fly man was 'the blue stocking of the angling world').

Fourth, personalities mostly appear in the form of biographical appreciations and obituaries. Thus H C Pennell (erratically hyphenated in the FG and, indeed, also in his own writings) and Frank Buckland (1885), J R G Maitland, Archibald Young, Ewen M Tod (1886) and John Younger (1891, 1895, many years after his death) all received notices (it is not quite clear why, except to fill up space). More interesting is a piece by 'Helvellyn' (FG, 1890, 20, pp. 204–5), entitled, 'A Trio of Famous Anglers'. It refers to a poor photograph purporting to be of A Russel (past editor of *The Scotsman* and a friend of Tom Stoddart), A Bertram (a journalist and presumably J G Bertram author of *A Guide to the Tweed* (1858)) and W C Stewart ('an Edinburgh tea merchant'). All three were said to be dead, which indeed they must have been for decades. This provides one of the very few fragments of biographical information published about W C Stewart (see Chapter 6). Obituaries in the volumes that I scanned were few and not very informative: Tom Stoddart (1880), Francis Francis (1887), Davies Hodge (1889), Edward Hamilton (1889). There was also a short but striking series in 1889–93 about 16 notable Scottish 'fishermen' or ghillies. These were dull little articles indeed but with some splendid pictures that could have been marvellously translated into pen and ink by Leech.

Fifth and finally, new inventions, tackle tips, DIY and so forth figured in most issues. A catalogue would be vast and dull. It will suffice to note that split cane rods, dressed silk lines and eyed hooks were all being pushed in the early 1880s. Innumerable spinners were promoted (some reversible to offset the potential horrors of the Malloch reel); there was an interesting discussion of the leader/cast/collar nomenclature matter, which is still with us today; waterproof clothing abounded; the correspondence pages covered an extraordinary array of ideas from silly to sensible; writers promoted untested knots, then as now; double-hooked midges (that is, side-by-side doubles) were apparently invented twice, in 1882 by R C Steven and praised by Marston and again, much later, by John Forrest and praised by Tod in 1897. Tod later promoted them in his book, explaining that the fact that the shanks could rotate was actually an advantage rather than a defect or drawback, as might have been thought. But, no matter if there was some nonsense, the old FG still makes splendid reading on equipment. My favourite item, oft repeated and not especially Scottish, is the indefatigable Messrs Burberry's 'double-rimmed fishing helmet'; it was a gabardine hat with a double brim, of which the top half could be lifted to provide a circular trough into which casts could be securely wound. It seems doubtful to me whether it would preserve either casts or heads in good condition.

12
Poesy and Anecdotage

T his chapter is a mixture of observations on bad verse and indifferent anecdotes, all relating to Scottish angling but none of much interest. The slightly pejorative tone of the chapter title is quite deliberate. I shall begin with the verse.

Tom Stoddart, though an ardent scribbler, was at best an indifferent poet. John Waller Hills' (1821) remark that Stoddart 'lives however in his verse rather than his prose' is, to me, incomprehensible, unless Hills had very odd literary tastes. Nowadays, at least, Stoddart's verse and that of his circle is justly forgotten but his angling prose survives very well. And scanning the *Noctes* revealed no verse that I thought interesting, unless to excite the reflection that there is often more poetry in a few lines of Hogg's reported speech than in dozens of rhyming couplets by lesser men. I give an example in Chapter 3.

If Stoddart was a poor poet, the rest were bad to terrible. Alas, the terrible ones are not quite bad enough to scale the heights of good–bad poetry achieved by William McGonagall; only very rare passages are so awful as to be worth quoting but there are a few to follow. In approximate chronological order, Robert Liddell ('Sexagenarian' – how they loved pseudonyms!) wrote verses which came out erratically in 1867, 1871 and 1888 under the general title *The Lay of the Last Angler*; I gave up trying to understand dates, editions and titles and they do not matter anyway. Here and there Liddell approaches McGonagall and concludes with the immortal couplet:

> So I'll laugh too for I confess
> My outing was a great success.

The Songs of the Edinburgh Angling Club (Anon., 1858, 1878), especially the second edition, has some interesting but confused observations on the history of the Club and its Robin's Nest at Fernielee; it also has some quite attractive drawings and vignettes and a lot of terrible verses. The second edition contains the following lines on p. 155:

> Our Secretary Stewart,
> The King of Anglers he,
> Who floored Sir Cholmondeley Pennell,
> The 'Typical Cockney'.

I think there can be no doubt that this refers to the immortal William C Stewart but he died in 1872, six years before this edition in which, elsewhere, the secretary is identified as one, Menzies. No matter, Pennell (1837–1915) was always a good subject for a Scottish gibe but I would like to know whether the versifier knighted him out of ignorance or derision; a fictitious knighthood would be a good Scottish joke, I suppose. William Forsyth ('William o' Ye West', of course) wrote *A Lay of Loch Leven* (1877) that contains many pages of terrible verse about a St Mungo's Angling Club excursion to the place, written in a weird mixture of 'refeened' English and pseudo-Burns. John Anderson's (1885) *Autumn Gleanings or Ears of Barley* is a little book of appalling Victorian wind, including verses. John Dougall's *Angling Songs* (1901) start with an intolerably twee piece on 'the bonnie wee trootie' and end with some verse drama on Robert Bruce. The author is not to be confused with James Dougall, a proper angler (Chapter 7). Duncan Fraser did at least write some decent anecdotes, referred to later in this chapter. His *Angling Songs from Border Streams* (1907), however, seems to be a collection of dim verses, probably all by Fraser himself, collected from periodicals such as *The Scotsman*. Alas, the pictures, both half-tones and vignettes, are also poor.

The two Fergusons, James R and Malcolm (son and father), complete the dismal list. Their book *The Versatile Scot* (1911) is mostly anecdotage, with sentimental home-thoughts from abroad (JR having emigrated to the USA). But it is mentioned here for a closing verse:

> Oh! The glorious rolling Dochart,
> I love thee more and more,
> Each time I tread thy grassy banks
> And bag my bradan mor.

How is that for 'roseate fiction'? There are salmon in the Dochart and I have seen a few and certainly heard of poaching. But it must be nearly the worst river in Scotland for bradan, mor or otherwise. A few are said to be surreptitiously 'cleeked' in the upper burns and in the pool below the bridge in Killin, isolated when the water falls low. Curious to relate, Stoddart, in the *Rambles* (1866), thought the Dochart quite a good salmon river, which perhaps it was, once upon a time. He and Wilson were certainly fond of it.

Though nearly all the poems are dreadful, one author classifies as bad–good or good–bad (I am never quite sure which). That author is William McGonagall, Poet and Tragedian, Irish by origin but for many years a distinguished resident of Dundee. Fortunately, he was no angler so there seems to be only one possible quotation, as follows, on Loch Leven (where else?):

> Beautiful Loch Leven, near by Kinross
> For a good day's fishing the angler is seldom at a loss
> For the Loch it abounds with pike and trout
> Which can be had for the catching, without any doubt;
> And the scenery around it is most beautiful to be seen,
> Especially the Castle wherein was imprisoned Scotland's
> ill-starred Queen

I shall now turn to the anecdotage. It is better than the poesy but I think that angling anecdotes always come best from anglers whose other writings proclaim them to be experts. The blethery kind are rarely either expert or entertaining. They appear in approximate chronological order.

Charles St John wrote two books (1846, 1849, 1884 etc) but they are the all-too-frequent nineteenth-century mixture of reprints, revisions and retitles. They are mostly about shooting but with some natural history and angling, including the memorable observation that 'Loch Leven trout are famous throughout Scotland'. Andrew Young's book of 1857 was written from Invershin out of local knowledge of the North. He rather liked fancy spinners for trout and thought that 'backing up' a salmon pool was 'a reprehensible practice' (why?). James C Walter (who tended to call himself James Conway) wrote poor, blethery stuff (1861, 1902) about shooting and fishing from a haunt in Brighton. He clearly had fished fairly widely but went in for 'gentle readers' and scraps of Latin. John Leech, the immortal cartoonist, did not write anecdotes; he drew them and Mr Briggs' fishing excursions (1861) are superb.

Leech's book (n.d., 1861 in the NLS catalogue) was reproduced from drawings in *Punch*, wherein Mr Briggs also suffered equestrian misfortunes. Mr Briggs was a southern *nouveau riche* doing the right thing and about half the drawings in Leech's book refer to his Scottish misfortunes. Francis Francis (1874, p. 255) identifies the spot, on the Tay, of Mr Briggs's final triumph over adversity.

A tale oft-told, though of no great intrinsic interest, should be repeated here. In 1854, Canon Greenwell of Durham, a keen Tweed fisher, took specimens of an olive dun to James Wright of Sprouston. Wright tied a very successful pattern later immortalised as Green-well's Glory by Mr Brown, the schoolmaster of Sprouston (Tom Stewart, 1962–73, pt. 1, p. 12). There are also some enchanting drawings of the troubles that befall tourists in Cole and Ralston (1898).

I mentioned the anonymous *Songs of The Edinburgh Angling Club* earlier for the bad verses; the second edition (1878) is clearly in serious error as to W C Stewart but does give an account (accurate?) of the early history of the club from 1847. The Braithwaites, father and son (George F and Cecil, respectively) are of marginal interest. George was a Westmoreland man who fished the Borders and knew Tom Stoddart; Cecil fished often and widely in Scotland, from 1878 to 1922 and certainly caught lots of fish. Edwards-Moss seems to have been an Englishman who fished the Borgie–Loyal system one year and was knowledgeable about fisheries management. One of the better sets of anecdotes was published in a series of three volumes by the Manchester Anglers' Association (1880, 1883; 1882; 1894). Much of the content is not at all Scottish but enterprising Mancunians certainly travelled, caught fish and wrote. There are pieces about Sutherland and Tweed in volume 1, about Tweed and Don in volume 2 and about Loch Leven, Lochaber, Braemar, Ythan, Orchy and Awe in volume 3. The author of the last piece (C P Roberts) blamed Lord Breadalbane (probably quite unfairly) for introducing pike to Loch Tulla and thence to Loch Awe; but he agreed that some of the Awe pike were big ones. Pike, of course, were native far north of Tulla in Thornton's time and everyone likes to blame the Campbells for something.

Many works published in this century go back to experience of angling in the last. Gathorne-Hardy's articles, reprinted in 1900, are mostly about shooting but he caught salmon in small Argyllshire rivers. Ernest Briggs fished Galloway waters with his brothers for many years. His anecdotes (1908) are agreeable and his water-colours chocolate-boxy but attractive. Duncan Fraser, besides the verses referred to earlier, also wrote two books of anecdotes (1895, 1900; 1911). The first contains mainly pedestrian tales about excursions, mostly to Yarrow and Ettrick, interspersed with bad verses and indifferent pictures. The second is more interesting but hardly memorable. As well as a few good quotations from Meg Dodds and Mrs Mitchell (Tibby Shiel's daughter), he writes a humorous tale about a visiting Colonel who asked the local Minister to dine on an 'eighty-pound salmon', a twelve-pound fish which was all that he got from an eighty-pound beat. *Tout ça change?*

There are more miscellaneous anecdotes, none very exciting, in Aflalo (1913, Lady Evelyn Cotterell's salmon fishing), J M Brown (1893), W S Brown (1909), Gathorne-Hardy (1898), and G H H Hutchinson (1871, 1875). Hutchinson was a regular visitor to the Hebrides and interested in water control and fisheries management. A G Bradley (1915) fished mostly in England and Wales but knew the Borders a little from about 1875. Philip Geen's books (1905, 1907) are agreeable but have little Scottish content beyond recurrent excursions to the River Lyon. Wilfred Morris's books (1929, 1934) are readable blether, with some tales about Border angling, Tweed worthies and the remark that the dry fly, rare in the 1890s, really only became established in the 1920s; it took some time for Frederick Fernie to make his mark.

13
Summary

T his book is, in effect, about sporting fishing in Scotland in the nineteenth-century. Vast quantities of pike, perch and eels and diverse sea fish must have been taken for sporting and commercial reasons but their capture has gone almost unrecorded. Moreover, the sporting salmonid fishes were also taken in quantity for sale, though those that have been recorded on this subject have no place in this book. But it might be useful to recall that no salmon stream lacked its nets and other 'engines' and that even trout (as in Loch Leven) were a valued commercial resource. In addition a few men actually made their livings by angling, as did one of the later masters of the rod, David Webster. At least, it is clear that the record is very selective and certainly very incomplete: fly fishing for salmonid fishes written about by an educated minority predominated.

The nineteenth-century in Scotland saw sundry changes of which I consider the following to have been the most conspicuous. The points referred to all emerge in preceding chapters; many of them come out in books by J W Hills (1921) and C V Bark (1992), while several technical points about the history of tackle are drawn from Courtney-Williams's excellent book (1945).

First, the century saw a great surge of interest in sporting fishing from what seems to have been very little around 1800. Perhaps Thornton was a bit of an oddity and he mixed shooting and falconry with what we should now regard as rather unsporting fishing methods. By the end of the century, when there must have been thousands of anglers in action, there was still a great deal of poaching but 'sportingness' was a much clearer concept.

Second, the general biology of the salmonids was poorly understood in 1800 but had been sorted out securely in a few decades and fisheries management, based firmly upon fish biology, had made a good start by the end of the century. In these activities, both research and development, Scotsmen played prominent parts. One result was that Loch Leven trout and Scots salmon went round the world (while rainbows from North America did the same, of course).

Third, the surge of interest just mentioned was accompanied by the development of scores of clubs and of competitive angling. In the latter activity, Loch Leven figured prominently but was not universally loved, then as now. Like them or not, clubs and competitions exist and many anglers participate; Scotland was a key area for their development.

Fourth, over the century, there was a marked decline of native salmonid stocks, caused, presumably by a combination of catching, pollution and more or less benign environmental change such as land drainage (Stoddart hated it, whatever the agricultural attractions). But perhaps we should recall that salmon stocks have always been characterised by fluctuations and their imminent demise has often been announced. Of the decline of trout, though, there can be no real doubt and most British anglers, Scots included, depend in effect upon stocking for their fishing; the ten-pound baskets of wild brownies of Stewart's days disappeared decades ago.

Fifth, part of the reason for increased catching must have been increased populations of people and hence increased demands for commercial fish (encouraging poaching as well as legitimate fishing). But part must also have lain with the great improvements in communications effected by the railway developments of the 1850s onwards. Before 1860, travel in the north of Scotland was quite hard going; after 1870, the railways provided convenient starting points for angling only a day or so from London and hours away from the Scottish cities.

Sixth, if the railways opened up the remoter parts of the land to anglers, English visitors benefited as much as or more than Scots. Sporting tourism became a major industry and remains so to this day; but fishing was generally subsidiary to shooting in the nineteenth-century, so the trout went with the deer or the grouse to wealthy gentlemen who rented estates. This still happens but more and more water has become accessible to hotels and visitors, an inexorable trend seemingly accompanied by ever-growing bureaucratisation and technology-based management.

Seventh, the nineteenth-century literature is plainly concentrated on the Border waters, especially on the Tweed and, to a lesser extent, on the Clyde. The reason is presumably that these waters are where

75

educated local anglers (from Edinburgh especially) fished and about which they later wrote. So the emphasis on traditional Border fishing tactics is no surprise; it is inevitable and the scarcity of comment on the Highlands and on indigenous northern fishing practices seems, in retrospect, perfectly predictable. I remarked in Chapter 8 on the lack of mention of the marvellous Sutherland limestone lochs and their huge trout, even by knowledgeable tourists such as Archibald Young in 1880; I suspect that the locals knew about them but were not telling or were prevented by a language barrier from doing so; or maybe the visitors just did not bother to ask?

Eighth, the Scottish literature of the century is very rich indeed, as J W Hills pointed out, but there was little technical innovation native to Scotland. Methods were essentially conservative and such changes as were adopted over the 100 years were mostly borrowed from abroad. William C Stewart, it is true, was an influential proponent of revised methods of trouting but even his ideas were essentially derivative and did not wholly prevail in real-life practice. But it should also be recalled that, though the literature tends to concentrate on fly fishing, vast numbers of Scottish trout and salmon were taken on various baits and spinners. Nowadays, pejorative labels tend to attach to such practices but all the best nineteenth-century Scottish writers had perfectly easy consciences about worms, minnows and parr tails (even if salmon roe was beginning to attract adverse notice).

Ninth and last, even if such technical innovations were largely borrowed, the Scottish angling literature of the century was both copious and important, as J W Hills argued, surely correctly. The more important innovations are worth listing, and are listed below. Many were finally influential, Scottish conservatism and slowness to adopt notwithstanding.

Technical innovations characteristic of the nineteenth-century, many having earlier roots, were as follows. Most of them have emerged in preceding chapters of this book. Courtney-Williams's book (1945) provides some good historical detail and scanning the *Fishing Gazette* gives a 'feel' for the matter in the latter years of the century.

First, there was a trend for shorter and ferruled rods made of foreign materials, in place of the standard, gigantic spliced weapons made of domestic woods. Imported hardwoods (notably lancewood and greenheart) emerged in the earlier years of the century and were widely used around 1840. (Angling possibly owes something to harbour engineering, which favoured greenheart). There were numerous British split-cane rods from about 1800 onwards but these were not successful and the great change came about 1870, with the rapid adoption of the American hexagonal design. William Stewart (in the 1850s) was a greenheart man and Hamish Stuart (in the 1890s) used a Hardy Hotspur.

Second, the horsehair lines of Stoddart's day must have been horrible things indeed (though David Webster persisted with them at the end of the century). But the use of silk went back to the eighteenth-century, though it took a long time to displace hair. In Scotland, silk–hair mixtures were frequent and must have been almost as nasty as pure hair to handle, shoot and cast. But oil-dressed, pure silk lines (another American invention) prevailed and, by mid-century, Stewart and Harvie-Brown were in no doubt of their superiority. Their success must have been linked to the adoption of silkworm gut casts ('leaders'), of upstream styles (whether with wet or dry fly) and of relatively short, stiff rods that necessitated shooting line.

Third, plenty of fish were caught on horsehair casts, which had the advantage of not rotting easily. But hair was weak and the new-fangled silkworm gut, known but generally adopted only when the art of 'drawing' it was understood, was the natural complement to the silk line. It prevailed virtually everywhere by the end of the century (David Webster again notwithstanding!). 'Drawing' gut, incidentally, was not a matter of stretching it in the initial preparation but, rather, of cutting it down from an initially irreducible thickness to uniform thin strands.

Fourth, all trout flies and many salmon flies were tied on eyeless hooks with horsehair or gut incorporated. Untold numbers of flies and fish must have been lost because something rotted or broke or pulled out. Salmon flies often had whipped-in eyes of twisted gut before mid-century but trout flies tied to gut persisted well into the this century. (I first fly-fished with such in the late 1930s, using standard four-fly casts, reach-me-downs from an angling uncle.) However, eyed hooks started to emerge in the 1860s and dominated from the 1880s. For trouting, the increasing tendency to match nature, whether wet or dry, soon ensured the permanent dominance of the eyed fly. As a minor sidelight on trout flies, side-by-side 'wee doubles' were mentioned above and promoted by Ewen Tod. The early ones (see Chapter 11) were whipped together but the hook makers have been selling the brazed version in diverse sizes for very many years now; they still seem to be much more favoured, in larger sizes, for salmon and sea trout than for trout, despite Tod's advocacy and old Loch Leven practice. (Parenthetically, small sizes are easily and efficiently made nowadays by taking advantage of the modern adhesives that were unavailable to Tod; they are far cheaper than the purchased article and perfectly effective.)

Fifth and finally, the dry fly, specifically designed to represent a mature ephemerid or sedge and cast to float over the nose of a feeding fish, made erratic appearances in the early nineteenth-century. Origins were probably on the Dove and/or in south-western England and the method was widely adopted by the 1860s. It was associated with the use of the short rod, the silk line, the gut cast and the eyed hook, in fact all the 'modern' paraphernalia. In England, its use became wrapped up in a weird theological dogma ultimately centred on Hampshire (where a nymph sub-dogma was later added). Scotland was bothered by none of this theology and there is no reason that I know of to assert, as a few writers have, that Scottish anglers were ever 'really' dry fly fishers before the practice became established in the south. Even the usually sensible Fernie made some silly remarks about Stewart having been 'really' a dry fly fisher. In practice, there must have been some Scots awareness in the 1870s but enthusiasm spread slowly and sporadically and the method was explicitly promoted only from the early twentieth-century onwards. It was generally held, then as now, to have a useful place both on stream and loch. This was no doubt perfectly sensible. Dry fly fishing has its charms but it has never been a matter of dogma in Scotland. So sensible anglers adopt the pragmatic attitude well stated by Francis Francis as long ago as 1867: if it works, use it. Much later, Robert Bridgett saw the point, as he saw most angling points, perfectly clearly.

And that, I think, is as much as it seems to be useful to say by way of summary. It contains nothing very dramatic or surprising, though it does bear upon what is one of the richest bodies of angling literature ever identifiable as such. I have had great pleasure reading it; I hope others may be interested enough by this book to go and do some searching, reading and thinking for themselves. I have explored what I take to be many interesting questions but can not pretend to have solved all the problems.

Anthology

There has been much anthologising in the angling literature but few of the pieces that follow have ever appeared elsewhere. One simply could not illustrate the themes of this book by reference to existing anthologies. So that must be the justification for presenting yet another set of angling extracts. I first viewed the task of composing the collection with some dismay but, in practice, it turned out to be remarkably interesting and I was spurred on by Mr Colin McKelvie's encouragement.

All the quotations are from works cited in the text and bibliography of this book and they are virtually entirely unedited. I chose the extracts as being characteristic of the authors and illustrative of their practices, interests and styles. Some are brief, pithy and practical: others diffuse and not a little verbose. But if that's how the authors were, I was content to show it.

After various efforts to invent some logical arrangement of contents, I gave up and adopted an alphabetical listing by the author, which at least is simple and unambiguous. A glance at the introductory list will tell the reader who is there and what works are represented. The dates stated are of the copies actually used; some are early or first editions and some are not. (See Bibliography)

I suspect that few readers will want to read the anthology straight through but I hope it will be found to complement the text satisfactorily. For example, some will find it acceptable to read a piece of text and follow up with quotations from that specific author.

List of Contents of Anthology

25. The Stanley water on the Tay
26. Angling on Loch Awe

Grimble, A 1902. *Shooting and Salmon Fishing*
27. Good and bad salmon fisheries
28. Playing a salmon
29. Bait fishing for salmon

Hamilton, E 1884. *Recollections of Fly Fishing*
30. Playing a salmon
31. Salmon fly patterns

Harvie-Brown, J A 1898. *The Wonderful Trout*
32. Up-stream casting analysed
33. Vision and behaviour of trout
34. Always up-stream for trout
35. Baits and illegal methods for trout

Hicks, J 1855. *Wanderings*
36. Trouting in Loch Urigil
37. A Highland boat at Altnacealgach

Knox, R 1854. *Fish and Fishing in the Lone Glens of Scotland*
38. Biology of Loch Leven trout
39. Coarse fish in Lochmaben and the Annan

Lang, A 1895. *Angling Sketches*
40. Confessions of a duffer
41. A mysterious figure in Border hills

MacVine, J 1891. *Sixty-Three Years Angling*
42. An ungentlemanly angler
43. A salmon under the ice
44. Poachers' manners and morals
45. Trolling for salmon in Loch Tay
46. The author's superior skill and knowledge

Scrope, W 1921. *Days and Nights of Salmon Fishing*
47. Salmon fishing disasters
48. Wading the river
49. Casting and fishing the salmon fly
50. Salmon fishing needs strength rather than patience
51. Playing a large salmon
52. A Tweed baillie wi' a conscience
53. *Si non, quocunque modo*

Stewart, W C 1958. *The Practical Angler*
54. Angling is healthy
55. Fishing to catch fish
56. A stiff rod is essential
57. The skill of James Baillie

58. To fish upstream is essential
59. The errors of 'downstreamers'
60. Scottish trouting superior to English
61. Concentrate on the matter in hand
62. Worming is a summer sport
63. A fancy minnow tackle
64. Loch fishing is easy but not so tiring
65. Troll if you must.

Stoddart, T T 1847. *Angler's Companion*
66. Waders especially for the older angler
67. Trout flies simplified
68. Fishing the worm upstream
69. Salmon roe for trout sometimes justified
70. A gigantic eel from Tweed
71. 'Snatching' salmon in the Dochart at Killin

Stoddart, T T 1866. *Angler's Rambles*
72. Miscellany of snippets from the Rambles
73. In difficulties on the Spey
74. Stoddart's hatred of the pipes
75. Lost near Loch Lyon
76. On the river Dochart
77. Fly tying extemporised
78. Loch Laggan with Wilson
79. Boyhood trouting near Edinburgh, ca 1825
80. Wind-lines on Loch Luichart
81. Flies tied for the Professor by James Wright
82. Tibby and her hospitable house
83. Conviviality at Tibby's place
84. Stoddart's biggest Fish and others on Tweed
85. Superior eating quality of perch
86. Need to protect parr

Stuart, H 1899. *Lochs and Loch Fishing*
87. 'Upwards of 200 lakes'
88. Poaching and a close-time in Scotland
89. The rainbow trout favoured
90. The importance of a good boat
91. Flies, fished deep and shallow
92. Insists on small flies
93. Timing the strike
94. Dry fly may have uses on canals

Thornton, T 1896. *A Sporting Tour*
95. The great perch of Loch Lomond

96. Big trout from Loch Tay

Tod, E M 1903. *Wet Fly Fishing*

97. Dry fly has some uses in Scotland
98. The wet fly ever up-stream
99. The perfect rod
100. Wet flies should be wet
101. Slowly and quietly upstream
102. Reels and 'smashes'
103. Three trout at a time but precariously
104. 'Wee doubles' promoted

Webster, D 1885. *The Angler and the Loop Rod*

105. A long spliced rod preferred
106. Tapered horse-hair line
107. Accurate casting with the 'strap'
108. Always fish up-stream
109. How to cast
110. Worming the burn up-stream
111. Grayling held in contempt

Wilson, J 1840. *The Rod and the Gun*

112. Fishing the shore of the loch

Younger, J 1864. *River Angling*

113. Flies emerge from maggots
114. Always upstream for trout
115. A large, two-handed rod
116. A big, spliced rod preferred
117. 'Tighten' rather than 'strike'

1. R B Begg 1874
The drainage of Loch Leven in 1830–32

The drainage operations were fully completed towards the end of December 1830, and on the 25th of that month the waters of Lochleven were for the first time allowed egress by the 'new cut'. This operation was one requiring the exercise of considerable care and caution, as the waters then stood nearly 4½ feet above the top of the sluice, and any sudden rush would have occasioned very serious damage. The waters were allowed to subside gradually at the rate of from 1½ to 3 inches daily, until the loch attained its present level. Of course a great change in the appearance and extent of the loch was the immediate result: large tracts of sand were all along the shore (especially on the east side) left dry; the islands were much increased in size – the Inch or St Serf's alone having had from sixty to seventy acres added to it; the Paddock Bower was joined to the mainland, and three small islets which had never before been able, even in the driest seasons, to raise their heads above water, now plainly asserted their position. These changes could not fail to be attended with serious derangement in the old-established and favourite 'sets' or trout-netting stations; and it is somewhat surprising to find that the net-fishing in the season immediately following the reduction of the level of the lake was an unusually successful one. One of the witnesses before the Jury Court (John Carmichael), who was then a fisherman in the employment of the tacksman, states in his evidence that the year 1831 'was the best fishing season he had ever seen; that one haul in a day was often sufficient fishing for all that was wanted, and at the sets called Powmill and Prap they usually got about twenty-four dozen of trout at one haul. In 1832 they got sometimes good sets in "The Hems" – at one time eleven dozen of trout at one haul. In 1832 there was a falling off, and in 1833 it was still worse – would only get two dozen at a set, and often less.' This witness's statement is

THE

LOCHLEVEN ANGLER.

BY

*AN EX-PRESIDENT OF THE KINROSS-SHIRE
FISHING-CLUB.*

"*Douglas.* . . . But row towards St Serf's Island,—there is a breeze from the west, and we shall have sport,—keeping to windward of the isle, where the ripple is strongest."—THE ABBOT.

KINROSS:
GEORGE BARNET, HIGH STREET.
EDINBURGH AND GLASGOW: J. MENZIES & CO.
1874.

substantially corroborated by another of the tacksman's fishermen (John White), who states, in addition, that in 1831 they took 'at the Prap and Powmouth sets from thirty to forty dozen trout at two hauls, and in 1832, at the set called Jummock's Deep, near Old Manse of Orwell, they got thirty or thirty-one dozen at one haul.'

2. R B Begg 1874
Angling in Loch Leven in the later 19th Century

In the course of these observations allusion has been already made more than once to the fact that angling on Lochleven, although so very generally practised now, is comparatively of recent introduction. Until within the last twenty-five years there prevailed a general belief that the trout in Lochleven would not rise to the fly, and apparently this belief had existed, if not always, at least from an exceedingly remote period. No allusion whatever to the practice of angling is to be found in any of the earlier notices of the loch, and in so far as regards the earlier part of the present century, and the greater portion of last century, it is well known that angling was very rarely attempted. That it was seldom attended with even moderate success at and prior to the partial drainage of the loch, is evident from the remark which Mr James Wilson, the naturalist – himself an enthusiastic angler and a well-known master of the gentle craft, and one who had repeatedly essayed his skill on Lochleven – introduces into his evidence before the Sheriff Court in 1840. 'It is owing,' he says, 'to the superabundance of natural food that no trout in Scotland, where the actual number is so great, are so difficult to raise with the artificial fly. That their number is actually very great may be inferred from the fact that the loch is fished (with the net) continuously for eight months in the year without any apparent diminution in their numbers, and that twenty dozen and upwards are sometimes taken at a single haul.' This belief that the trout in Lochleven would not rise to the lure does not appear to have been a mere vague or unfounded one, nor to have been arrived at without being repeatedly put to the test; for the general lack of success did not deter many an enthusiastic and skilled sportsman from again and again patiently and perseveringly plying his favourite art on the tempting but delusive waters of the loch. From our own personal recollections we can particularise two very experienced veteran anglers connected with Kinross-shire, who, about thirty years ago, frequently and regularly, at different periods of the year, and for year after year in succession, devoted much time and patience to fly-fishing on Lochleven, and their take seldom exceeded a couple of good trout apiece, and they considered themselves most exceptionally fortunate it amounted even to that. The extreme rarity of a fair basket in days of yore may be gathered from the following paragraph, which was considered worthy of a prominent place in the *Perthshire Advertiser* of June 26, 1844: 'Lochleven Trout – Angling. – On Friday the 7th June 1844, two young sportsmen from Edinburgh caught with the fly 17 trout, weighing in all thirteen pounds – one fish additional was taken with the minnow. The day, we may mention, was drizzly and cloudy throughout. We mention the above, as the take on this occasion exceeds what has been known for upwards of forty years. An experienced friend informs us, however, that while occasionally, and only occasionally, from two to three trouts may be taken with the rod, anglers are generally altogether unsuccessful. The same friend informs us that the late Sheriff Skelton, a native of Kinross-shire, and well acquainted with the sport, on one solitary occasion killed in one day sixty-two good trouts.' Such appears to have been the unfavourable light in which angling on Lochleven continued to be regarded until about the year 1850, when a complete and utterly unaccountable change in the habits of the trout and the character of the loch unexpectedly developed itself. Instead of the trout continuing to be, as they had hitherto been, extremely shy and wary, they all at once began to rise readily to the lure, and numerous very heavy baskets were secured both with fly and minnow. How and by what cause this extraordinary change was produced has always been, and it is feared ever will remain, a mystery. It could scarcely have arisen from any diminution in the natural food afforded to the trout, as Mr Wilson's opinion above quoted would necessarily imply; for in that case the change would have proved as temporary in its duration as it was sudden in its event, unless, indeed, it is to be supposed that the decrease of bottom food was of such a very serious and permanent character as to leave its effects undiminished for nearly a quarter of a century, and certainly a change of that description could scarcely have come over the loch without its being traceable to some very decided and clearly perceptible local cause. Neither could this sudden inclination of the fish to rise to the artificial fly be the result of any material increase in the stock of trout in the lake; for if so, the net-fishings would also have become more productive than they had been in former years; whereas, from the statement already given of the yearly takes during the earlier portion of the present century, it will be seen that at that time when angling was generally unsuccessful, the loch was much better stocked with trout than it has ever been since. The change, from whatever cause arising, was not a gradual one, but was as sudden as it was complete; and the successful takes were no sooner announced than anglers from all parts of Scotland and England began to resort to the lake in considerable numbers, and these have continued yearly to increase. Lochleven became at once established as undoubtedly the best trouting lake in Scotland, and for upwards of twenty seasons it has continued to maintain its character as such. During that period, by far the greater number of trout taken from the lake have been caught with the rod – in season 1872 the proportion being 18,000 trouts caught with the rod, against little more than 2000 caught with the net; and in season 1873 there having been caught 13,394 trouts with the rod, against 596 caught with the net.

3. R B Begg 1874
An angling episode
on Loch Leven

'That has been an exciting little "spurt,"' said I, after matters had again settled down, and we had fished for some time without a rise. 'It's only a pity it did not last a little longer.'

'Yes,' said Palmer; 'or come somewhat oftener. But, hallo!' he added, as his fly was quietly sucked under water with only the slightest apparent commotion on the surface, and instantly his line ran out with a quick, prolonged strain, which sent his reel spinning as if it never would stop. 'What have we here? That's a trout, I'll be bound, that is worth our whole take put together. What a strong, vigorous pull he has, and how he keeps down in the water! I suspect it will take some time to bring that fellow into a tractable humour.'

Our attention was at once concentrated in Palmer's operations, and assuredly they were worth studying. His whole appearance, from the soles of his boots to the crown of his hat, indicated keenness and excitement; and as he stood holding his lithe and supple rod, and humouring, as far as he could, the rapid and sometimes eccentric movements of his trout, he would have formed an admirable artistic study of 'an angler thoroughly in his element.' The trout carried out an enormous length of line, and for what appeared to me to be a very long time, it kept up the most vigorous play, never allowing itself for a single moment to be brought near the surface of the water. Occasionally, when it was to all appearance exhausted, and Palmer with great dexterity and caution had shortened his line considerably, and was gently guiding the trout to the upper air near the boat, it would suddenly arouse itself once more to new efforts, and again and again it darted off far to leeward. This was tantalising, for the strain on the rod and line indicated clearly that the trout was an unusually large one, and from the first the boatmen and myself had stood intently watching for a glimpse of it. At length our patience was rewarded; for after many disappointments the trout was fully brought to view, and shortly thereafter it was in course of being gently towed on the surface of the water, lying quietly on its side, with its rich yellow belly fully displayed. I had often heard of the Lochleven trout being caught of considerable size, but this was the first that I had ever seen exceeding in weight two pounds at the utmost. It was truly a magnificent trout, apparently fully five pounds in weight; and, alike in form and colour, it was simply faultless.

4. R C Bridgett 1922
Necessity for the dry fly

T he angler's rest ceased with the first grand leap, his rod has awhile been active; but, though he finds its labours not quite without reward, he is perplexed with doubts and vexed with questionings.

Why should his fly disappear beneath the surface, when the beautiful insect it copies sails the wave? Though it be an exact imitation in form, size, and colouring, can it give him faithful service when it errs in such a conspicuous and important particular? Why does it not remain in full view, bobbing to every wavelet, sitting naturally on the water, answering the wind and the current?

Will the wise and wary trout not look with suspicion upon his lure, made with infinite pains and skill though it be, and treat it with the contempt it merits? The younger fry, not yet versed in the wiles of man, and still unaware of the dangers that surround them, may accept the unnatural object without hesitation; but the older, experienced trout will flee from its vicinity.

With so much to persuade him the angler will retrieve his unsuccessful fly, which miserably fails to yield the sport that the pool can give, and the conditions allow; he will dry it carefully, anoint it with some preparation which will enable it to resist the water, and send it forth endowed with greatly increased capacity to compete with the living insects for the attention and acceptance of the eager trout. No longer will it be ignored, but at every subsequent shower of March Browns it will deceive a fish or two, and the basket will begin to grow agreeably heavy.

The only really wonderful fact about the dry-fly is that it was not invented first. Instead of being a development of the wet-fly, it should have been its precursor. Why did these old anglers, who have assisted so much by their study of the food of trout and by their laborious search for materials wherewith to copy the various species of flies, attend only to certain details, highly essential no doubt, and ignore the most important characteristic? Of course, in these far-off days trout were numerous and unsophisticated, and anglers were few, so that little thought was demanded; but even that fact does not excuse or explain the omission.

Some may respond that it is easy to be wise after the event. They should, however, note that the use of a floating fly was advocated at least seventy years ago, and that the idea has occurred to many anglers who had previously never read a single word about it or seen anyone using it. It is certainly surprising that the art of dry-fly fishing has taken so long to become well-known.

As long as trout are accustomed to see flies, living or dead, sailing on the surface of the water, and are willing to take them, so long must the angler take heed that his artificials behave in exactly the same way. Wherever trout have reached a degree of wariness sufficient to make them suspicious of a winged lure borne down beneath the surface in answer to a current or other force, then he must make sure that his fly will not be unnatural in action.

In some streams, thrashed every day by many anglers, it is a well-known fact that sport is generally poor during the summer months. It is commonly stated that the reason for this is that the trout are well-fed, and neither require nor desire food. With that some disagree, maintaining that the fish have had such abundance of insect-food that they are completely sated with it, and wish a change of diet. Acting on this assumption, they fish the worm in clear water and prove conclusively that the trout are very keen on food; but it does not follow that flies are temporarily out of favour.

On a cold day in July or on a warm summer evening, flies are plentiful, and trout will take them quite as greedily as at any other time. The fact is that flies never are unwelcome, but on certain days, particularly in summer, they are very scarce, conditions being not such as they prefer. It is very seldom indeed that on a river a hatch is not accompanied by a rise; but the trout have learned a lot during the spring, re-learned all that they forgot during the winter, and the result is that they are less easy to deceive.

The ordinary wet-fly is now practically worthless; but a dry-fly, if floated carefully over a feeding fish, is almost certain to produce a rise. Those anglers who object to natural baits of all kinds will find that a floating fly will bring to an end much of the disappointment they experience in the difficult days of July and August.

95

5. R C Bridgett 1922
On choice of dry flies

O f floating flies there is such an immense variety that the beginner in the art of dry-fly fishing must be perplexed and discouraged, when he is confronted by the almost endless array of patterns laid out for his inspection in the tackle-shop.

He cannot tell what to accept and what to reject; he may not know which specimens represent living insects and which are copies of purely imaginary flies. He is at a loss, and is forced to ask advice from the dealer. The latter will say regarding a particular pattern either that it is a good killer or that he sells a lot of it, one of which is perfectly true, for there are only two types of dry-fly, viz. one which appeals to fish, and one which attracts fishers.

The unfortunate beginner is therefore not assisted much towards a selection, and probably acquires a large stock, the majority of which he will never use.

The hosts of flies which are at home on our rivers, or pay them unpremeditated and undesired visits, have all been more or less faithfully counterfeited; but not content with these, some anglers have set their ingenuity to work, given their imagination free scope, and designed flies unlike anything in nature. The products of their skill are artistic creations very pleasing to the eye of the inexpert, who is charmed with the neatness of the workmanship, delighted with the colour scheme, and is apt to feel that at last he has within his reach the means which will render impossible an empty creel.

On putting to the test any one of his possessions, no matter how much it differs from any known insect, he will find that, provided he has oiled it and has not selected a day during which the trout have unanimously resolved to abstain from food, it will bring him at least a little sport, for the simple reason that the fish will see the fly on the surface, the place where they expect to see flies.

Almost any combination of silk and feather which floats will deceive a fish or two; but that fact, instead of justifying the invention of new patterns, shows its utter futility. A copy of the fly that is on the water, or was there yesterday, or would be if the conditions permitted, will prove far more acceptable than the most ingenious improvement upon nature ever designed, and therefore one who has little knowledge of dry-fly fishing should restrict himself to a few patterns such as are described below. When he becomes expert he will find them adequate for all his requirements.

We shall deal in the first place with the *Ephemeridæ*. As these flies of the upright wing exist in two distinct winged states, the sub-imago or dun, and the imago or spinner, it would appear almost necessary to have four artificials for each species in order that the two sexes in each state may be represented. If such detail were essential for every species, then the total number of patterns required by the angler would be formidable. As a matter of fact, however, many species exhibit only minute differences, and the sexes of the same species show so little variation in general appearance that the trout of the streams we have fished have not yet learned to distinguish between them. Their brethren of other rivers and countries may be more discriminating, but for some years to come, even on the most frequented Scottish waters, a copy of the female fly, dun and spinner, will satisfy the trout and all anglers, except the ultra-purist.

6. R C Bridgett 1922
On dressing dry flies

A fly dressed with double wings lasts for a longer time and accounts for a larger number of trout than one with single wings. After a fish is captured, the fly should be washed, dried, oiled, and dried again – for an absolutely dry fly is at times infinitely superior to all other – and then the fibres of the wing should be gently stroked into position. Such flies are mostly of use in spring and autumn, but on any cold day of summer a fleet of sub-imagines may be seen sailing down the stream, when of course the angler will at once take the hint.

It has been fashionable for a few years to imitate, or rather suggest, the wings of spent spinners by means of hackle-tips fastened on horizontally at right angles to the hook; for some time we contentedly used these extremely delicate lures and spoke in praise of them; but now we consider that there is a serious defect in their construction.

When the female imago has completed its life's work, it falls spent and exhausted on the water; its transparent wings lie spread out, in contact with and flat on the surface. In fact, they are invisible to an angler on the bank, but he will see them easily if he wades out and looks vertically down upon them.

The cock-hackles, which support, as they should, the imitation dun high in the water, cannot, however convenient it might be, accommodate us now by refusing to do likewise with the spent spinner; the wings cannot lie on the surface if the generally recommended cock-hackles are used. A careful application of the floating agent to the body and wings, but not the hackle, might make the fly a much more satisfactory lure; but it is difficult to prevent the liquid spreading to parts where its presence is not desired.

After a fairly long trial we have found a fly dressed in spider-fashion superior to the hackle-point spinner. Such patterns are very effective during the evening rise and also in low water in summer. The majority of spiders we have seen err in having too much and too long hackle, some of them, March Brown spiders particularly, being excellent miniatures of the brush of a chimney-sweep, but very unsatisfactory attempts to imitate a fly.

The conclusions arrived at are that, so far as the *Ephemeridæ* are concerned, the duns should be dressed with double wings and single cock-hackle, the spinners without wings and short, soft hen-hackle.

7. R C Bridgett 1922
Casting the dry fly

S ome anglers may prefer a calm to a downstream wind, but we most decidedly do not, except when the fish are rising very well. We object to walk from stream to stream, omitting the long flats and pools where, on a familiar river, we have had fine sport on other days, or where, on a new water, we are sure that good trout lie in wait; and that is what we feel constrained to do if the smooth surface of the water remains undisturbed by wind or feeding fish. If, however, a downstream wind causes a ripple, we can fish contentedly enough between the streams, even although no rise is in progress.

To put a fly straight across a strong wind calls for very little skill in the manipulation of the rod, therefore no matter from what direction the breeze comes, good casting and successful fishing are both easily possible. The angler faced with a downstream breeze should cast across it, and work his way gradually upwards. We have already pointed out the extreme deadliness of this cast in quick-flowing water, and again we give the warning that its virtues will all be thrown away, if the flies are allowed to float too far, or the line becomes too slack. It is rather difficult to keep in close contact with the fly as it floats down, because the wind blows out the line; a short journey for the fly and a low rod-point will help the angler materially.

As the dry fly fisher proceeds up the pool or stream, casting across the current and the wind, he will naturally be always endeavouring to put his fly a short distance, at least, upstream, and it will be surprising if he does not suddenly discover himself to be possessed of a new power, viz. ability to cast into the wind. It is easy to learn to overcome a gentle adverse breeze, and practise first under simple, and later under more difficult, conditions will in time make him indifferent to the wind and its direction.

It may assist him to be told that he should lower the rod on delivery parallel to the water, turn his hand sharply to the right, and bring it in towards his body. If he can attend to these points, and do each at the required moment, he has reached proficiency. Great force is unnecessary, and even fatal with this or any other cast; the rod should never be heard. Some anglers like to make the rod whistle in the wind, but such sounds merely indicate misplaced energy.

A gale makes fishing both unpleasant and tiresome and, when it blows downstream, it is the torment of the dry fly man. As he must fish, he should attempt to cast across it, and if his fly is blown farther down the current than he would like he need not worry; he may by walking keep up with his fly for a yard or more, before it begins to drag.

If he observes a trout rising, he should endeavour to float a fly down to it, while he himself remains stationary.

In a high wind fish seldom rise quietly, but usually hurl themselves upon the fly, taking no time to scrutinise it and accepting it greedily if its behaviour is above reproach. Sport is therefore sometimes surprisingly good, though conditions are all unfavourable to accurate placing.

Even the early writers on angling paid some attention to the direction of the wind as well as to its strength. Dame Juliana Berners in her *Treatise on Fishing with an Angle* enumerates several impediments which cause men to take no fish, and of these the last may be translated as follows: 'If the wind be from the North or North-east or South-east, fish will not commonly bite nor stir; the West and the South are very good, but of the two the South is the better.'

The Master, in his Epistle to the Reader, hopes that if he be an honest angler, the East wind may never blow when he goes a-fishing. The Book of St Albans gives the East wind as the worst of all. In addition, we have sundry old rhymes which proclaim the beneficial qualities of the South and West winds, and declare the East wind fatal to the angler's sport.

There are many anglers in Scotland who will disagree with these statements, or at least will accept them only with qualifications, and old Izaak himself, had he known Loch Leven, would probably have made a special exception of that water, which, it is generally agreed, fishes best in an East wind. Even yet the belief is very prevalent that trout will not rise well when the breeze is from that quarter; neither, we suppose, will larvæ move about with freedom or be inclined to change their state. If any loch or river yields good results under such a condition, it is looked upon as some wonderful exception which must be subjected to examination and explained away.

Attempts have in consequence been made to account for this supposed peculiarity of Loch Leven. It has been argued that, as an East wind is not so colder immediately it leaves the sea as it is after it has traversed many miles of the colder land, and as Loch Leven is near the East coast, a wind from the East is there not harmful in its effects.

This seems to make rather many assumptions: first, that a cold wind makes trout fast; secondly, that the East wind is warmer on the East coast than it is inland; thirdly, that the land is colder than the sea; and lastly, that whatever is not harmful is beneficial.

8. R C Bridgett 1922
An outing on Loch Lyon

On our arrival a very light, fitful breeze from the east was raising the tiniest of wavelets, and it seemed doubtful whether it would die away altogether or change round to the west. We decided to make use of the little there was, and proceeded to drift towards the mouth of the river, which enters at the head of the loch. This is really a delightful bit of water to fish, a fine curving bay, with shores of golden sand, fringed with reeds, certainly very promising water. The first drift produced only half a dozen fish, and these of meagre dimensions, but meantime the wind had freshened, so we pulled half-way down the loch to the Poachers' Point.

On both sides of this low-lying promontory there are grand bays, and we began to get what Johnnie termed the true Loch Lyon brand, fine yellow trout, full of fight, running from one-third to half a pound, with occasionally a rather better specimen. It was remarkable that no fish were showing, there being no hatch of fly, but, notwithstanding that fact, they seemed disposed to take anything that happened to come along. Using flies somewhat larger than standard Loch Levens, we cast before us, and the reels were screeching merrily and with agreeable frequency. Often we both were running fish simultaneously, and we were fortunate to be provided with two landing-nets.

The trout showed a preference for Peter Ross and the Butcher, but, as these happened to be respectively our tail- and bob-flies, their superior killing powers may have been due to their positions rather than to their own inherent value. Other flies which proved worthy of their place in the team were March Brown, Greenwell's Glory, Woodcock and Yellow. Sometimes the trout took the fly the moment it alighted on the water, sometimes the wily bob-fly worked across the waves had a fatal attraction, and occasionally it was only by sinking the flies considerably that we were rewarded. Whichever way they came the answering strike had to be forthcoming immediately, for the trout of Loch Lyon are very agile and can reject a fly instantaneously. When hooked they leap into the air or bore deeply, pulling with a strength which, considering their size, is phenomenal.

The bow-rod, after reaching the fateful number thirteen, had almost given up in despair of surpassing that total, when he raised two trout at the same moment and succeeded in landing both. As each of them was a half-pounder in perfect condition, he must have had quite an exciting time piloting both into the landing-net. After lunch sport was not quite so brisk, and at 4 p.m. the wind died away completely after coming true from the east for so long a time. The loch became a mirror, unbroken by the rise of any trout, so that fishing seemed to be labour in vain.

We counted the spoils, sixty-seven trout, which on being weighed later reached the respectable figure of 22 lb., so we decided to beach the boat and prepare for the homeward journey. Johnnie pleased us by remarking that it was the second best basket of the whole season, only five fish behind the record, which, moreover, had been made under better conditions, a fine steady breeze blowing all day from the west. We had only one regret, and that was that we had not been privileged to fish Invermearan Bay, reputed to be the best bit of the water, situated at the eastern extremity of the loch, but the omission was solely due to our distrust of the wind.

It is not advisable to come to conclusions after a single day's experience of a loch, and the practical hints which follow are those supplied by our boatman. We found his advice to be thoroughly sound. Small flies do not seem to have much attraction for the trout of Loch Lyon, except perhaps when the breeze is very light, and even under such conditions the size ordinarily used will prove to be equally serviceable. When a considerable wave is on, even larger flies, approaching sea-trout size, are advised, and it is then that the best sport is obtained and the best quality of fish captured.

Up till the end of July trout should be sought in the bays and round the shores in comparatively shallow water, but towards the end of the season they are to be found rising in deeper parts, even in the centre of the loch. Fine gut is not required, 2x thickness being sufficiently strong to tackle any trout one is likely to meet, but of course refinement in materials always meets with an increase of sport.

9. R C Bridgett 1922
Entomology on the loch

C onsequently I believe that some acquaintance with the
entomology of the loch is required. The angler, however, desires only so much, enough to enable him to fish
intelligently, and, as a necessary consequence, with greater success.
He has no wish, and he has no need, to become an expert
entomologist. He wants to catch trout, not to acquire, after much
laborious study, a multitude of scientific names, not to trouble
himself with microscopic distinctions. He wants, for example, to
be able to recognise at a glance, and name the different families of
flies and know their characteristics, so that he may compare notes
with his friends, and, in so doing, avoid confusion, which meantime,
though simple to avoid, is very prevalent. In addition to that,
acquaintance with a few species of each family will assist him
considerably.

Loch flies may be divided, well enough for the angler's purpose,
into three classes, viz., duns, caddisflies, and two-winged flies. They
are readily distinguished from one another. A dun is recognised at
once by its upright wings; these stand vertically at right angles to the
body, and, when the fly is at rest, they touch almost from base to tip.
Before the fly reaches this stage it has spent some considerable time
as an aquatic creature, a nymph, and after a period of varying
duration as a dun, it undergoes another change into the perfect
insect; a spinner it is then generally termed. After a brief experience of
this second aerial existence it falls exhausted on the surface, the wings
being then outstretched horizontally to the body and flat on the
water. The fish feed greedily on the insect in all its stages, nymph,
dun, and spinner, but from the trout's point of view the first is the
most important. By far the greatest part of the insect's life is passed
under water. At all times the nymph, if it ventures forth from hiding
at all, is liable to capture, but when it is about to undergo its
transformation it is most easily obtainable. Therefore the nymph
should likewise receive the greatest attention from the loch-fisher. 105

Everyone knows the caddis-fly and its larva, or rather the kind of home the larva builds for itself. The insect exists in only one winged state. The wings are four in number, the outer pair being much larger than the inner, and concealing them altogether when the insect is not flying. The wings cover the whole length of the body, projecting even beyond it, and they meet at their upper edges in an angle. The flies are more substantially built than duns, do not venture far from the water, and most, but by no means all, prefer the gloaming or the dark to the full light of day. The larval tubes are varied in shape and size, material and external ornamentation, and may be obtained from the bed of the loch or from weeds. When the larva is sufficiently developed, it leaves its tube and rises straight to the surface; when on the way its life is in danger, but, if it escapes the perils of the journey, it unfolds its wings, skates about for a time, and then flies off in a blundering sort of fashion. This procedure is not common to every species, but is characteristic of some. Owing to the fact that only for a short space of time is the larva obtainable by the fish and is in a state that can be copied, I consider that the fully fledged fly merits the principal notice.

Two-winged flies are an exceedingly numerous company, many of them being true aquatic insects with interesting life-histories, but rather too varied to investigate. Some larvæ are very retiring, burrowing in mud or concealing themselves amongst weeds; others move freely about, hanging at the surface or undertaking little voyages through the water. Gnats and midges are the chief members of this class, and both the larval and winged states are important. Some of them are so very minute as to defy imitation; the angler has therefore to content himself with a suggestion, the Badger Hackle for example, which, though not by any means a facsimile, effects its purpose very well indeed.

I am convinced that it is owing principally to the lack of really satisfactory imitations of the larvæ of duns and midges and also, to a smaller extent, to the fact that loch-fishers have been rather easy to please with representations of winged flies, that there are so many comparatively poor days on the loch. As soon as artificials bearing a closer resemblance to the living creatures are available, all that remains to ensure a great increase of sport is a general knowledge of the method of using them. The river-fisher has beautiful, life-like copies of flies to use. Why is the loch-fisher so easily satisfied? There are many days on the loch on which not a trout is seen breaking the surface, and flies on such occasions may be present and they may not; some of these days are quite good from an angling point of view and some are bad. Those that are good would be very much better if we could make and use the right type of lure, while the blank days would become very exceptional.

10. R C Bridgett 1922
The composition of the loch cast of flies

There is considerable difference of opinion as to the number of flies a cast should carry. Probably because the rules drawn up for various competitions on Loch Leven forbid the use of more than four flies on the cast, that number has become general there at all times and on other lochs as well. With the rest, for many years I fished with four flies, but some time ago I began to feel that the cast was thus somewhat overloaded. The flies were so close together that often I was unable to tell with certainty, when a rise came and was not accepted, which of the lower three flies had been honoured; of course, there was never any doubt regarding the bob-fly and its successes. Consequently what might have proved to be valuable information regarding the desires of the trout at a particular time was lost. I do not suppose that a fish is more likely to become suspicious when it sees four flies passing before it in procession than it will when only three are presented for its inspection; it may be even the more impressed, but, owing to the uncertainty mentioned, I have for most occasions reduced the number of flies to three. They divide up the available length more satisfactorily, giving a greater interval between one fly and the next, and another advantage which, though the expert may deem it none, the beginner is sure to appreciate, is that the entanglement of the cast into patience-destroying confusion will be a less frequent occurrence.

In special circumstances, e.g., where weeds are abundant, I use only two flies but, except when fishing the floating fly over rising trout or searching little clear spaces among reeds, I refuse to reduce the number to one solitary individual, and for this very good reason that I should thus be denying myself not only the pleasure of working the bob-fly but also the great sport that it is often capable of bringing. I once had the privilege of fishing a loch the trout in which average between three and four pounds. I secured one of 3½ lb. The cast carried three flies, and the possibility of having to play two fish at a time did not trouble me at all during the day. Had the thought crossed my mind, I should have made no alteration on the cast, because the sport of losing two such monsters would, it seems to me, be greater than that of landing one; in fact, I should welcome at any time such a rare opportunity. Perhaps those who fish only one fly on the cast do so, not because they are afraid of a double capture, but because they think that a second fly might interfere with the correct working of the first, or for some other reason. There is no doubt that the angler will always fish best when he employs methods in which he has most confidence.

If the gut has been previously well soaked, the making of a cast should, after practice, occupy only a very few minutes. The lengths of gut may be joined together by any one of the usual knots, and of these I greatly prefer that which is known as the blood-knot. My chief reason for that is that it provides a very simple and exceedingly neat method of attaching a dropper-fly, it being, of course, understood that the eyed-fly is used. Also the knot at which a fly is attached is no bigger than any other knot, whereas, if any other method known to me is used, the visibility of the cast is greatest exactly at those points where it should be least. The cast should be parallel up to the knot beyond the bob-fly; thereafter it may be tapered to the line, so affording stronger gut for the loop, the point at which friction is most severe. So infinitesimal is the amount of gut used in tying on an eyed-fly, that a dropper-point of quite satisfactory length can be fitted in succession with four or five flies before it becomes too short to be serviceable; the method recommended for making the cast is therefore not uneconomical.

11. R C Bridgett 1922
Choice and fishing of loch flies

The Teal and Green, an excellent tail-fly, does not quite belong to the same category as Peter Ross. I have before suggested that it owes its power to the similarity that exists between it and the larva of the green midge. As it may, however, rely on some other property still unknown to me, and as it is a proved killer from June onwards, I think it should be included in the stock of loch-flies. The following dressing answers very well: –

Teal and green – Body of green seal's fur, ribbed with oval silver tinsel, hackle of black hen, tail of golden pheasant tippet, and dark teal wing.

That brings us to what is probably the most deadly loch-fly ever invented, viz., the Butcher. Dressed with split wings well laid back, used on the bob, and made to trip across the waves, it is an exceedingly reliable fly on every loch that I have fished. It does well among rising trout, provided there is a fair breeze; its powers seem to become greater under sunshine except, of course, on Loch Leven. Even when trout are not breaking the surface at all, it is able to bring them up, and I think that, on these occasions, the fish are eagerly watching for flies. For this conclusion I can give no adequate reason; perhaps the Butcher happens to be just sufficiently conspicuous to excite curiosity without arousing suspicion. In any case it is very deadly. If winged in the ordinary way it is quite a good tail-fly, and used by many in this position with considerable effect. The dressing is: –

Butcher – Body of flat silver tinsel ribbed with oval silver, hackle of black hen, tail of red ibis, crow wing rolled and tied back.

Besides these there are dozens of other patterns all very lovely to look upon, and all capable no doubt of exciting the predatory instincts of trout, but not, one would imagine, likely to arouse the desire to eat. They are really too numerous to mention. I have possessed them, used them when in despair, killed trout with them, but I think that their usefulness is not of the same pronounced type as their beauty. Perhaps some anglers find one or more of them generally effective; it may be that they can put them through the correct evolutions, or that they know the conditions which bring out their peculiar qualities. These are certainly possibilities, but I have never happened to hear anyone say very much in favour of these lures.

It must be apparent that no fly can be worked correctly at all stages of the draw; that is an argument in favour of using more than one fly on the cast. When the lures alight on the water, at that moment they will all appear to the trout as flies just arrived from the air, and for such may be taken. As soon as that moment passes, the lures begin to sink, for the angler generally pauses, and should pause, before proceeding to bring them towards the boat. He is not only preparing for the backward cast, he is also fishing his flies. He may draw them slowly or quickly, at a uniform pace or in a series of jerks, by raising the rod, or by pulling in line with the left hand, or by an application of both methods simultaneously. Supposing that there are four flies on the cast, the lower two will be behaving more or less after the manner of nymphs and shrimps, while the remaining two will appear as flies, for the trout is probably unable to tell whether a fly is on, above, or just below the surface. After a time the bob-fly reaches the top, and it alone is then fished; it is to the trout a fly making efforts to escape from the water. Many of the rises to the bob are wild, or rather they only appear to be wild, the fish in their eagerness overshooting the mark or, troubled by reflections, making a mistake in aim.

Soon the rod loses command of the fly and another delivery must be made.

12. R C Bridgett 1926
Angling weather

T hunder is generally regarded as totally unfavourable to the angler, and certainly a close sultry atmosphere has such an enervating effect on him that it is reasonable to assume that trout are similarly rendered averse to exertion, but, when the storm breaks, sport becomes, sometimes at any rate, both fast and furious. One day remains a clear memory. It was spent on Loch Dochart. Heavy black clouds gathered beyond Strathfillan and slowly spread across the sky, until a darkness as of night fell over the country. Not a leaf stirred in the still air; the loch lay absolutely unruffled from shore to shore; not a ring of a rising trout disturbed the calm; the birds of the woods, the hills, and the reeds were silent. So certain was a storm on the way that all the boats but one came ashore, and all the anglers but myself hurried towards Crianlarich. A torrential rain poured down vertically on the loch. Thunder rolled among the rocks and crags of Ben More; lightning played around on every side. The sport was immense. In less than an hour, as quickly almost as it could be done, I had a dozen trout on board, all beauties, all far above the usual average. The river came down in high flood, soon rendering the loch muddy and unfishable; the mountain slopes were seamed with white; the burns were raging torrents. In several parts the road was under water; indeed I had been infinitely more comfortable on the loch than I was on the homeward way. Thereafter sport remained good for several days, perhaps because the trout had been thoroughly stirred up, but more probably because the loch was high, the weeds well covered, the fishing area increased. Only once have I found trout eager to rise when a thunderstorm was threatening. That was on Clyde. From one pool I took six pounds of trout to the dry fly; then the rains descended, and I said farewell to the generous place.

Many anglers express a great dislike for cold weather, and declare that it renders fly-fishing profitless. With that opinion I cannot wholly agree. In the earlier part of the season there is no doubt that a warm atmosphere is generally accompanied by a hatch of flies and a rise of trout, but it does not seem a necessary condition, for I have seen a strong burst of March Browns and a display of whole-hearted attention to them when snow was falling. In July I look upon a cold day as a promise of superior sport, and seldom is it that expectations are not realised. A hatch of duns is, one might venture to affirm, a certain occurrence, and the river-trout becomes very active. It is well known to a number of experienced river fishers that in July and August a boisterous day is the most likely to yield sport to the ordinary wet fly. The reasons for that are complex. The imperfections of the fly and the necessary attachment of gut are less conspicuous; the angler's presence is less easily detected, and it may be that the trout themselves are more unsuspecting than usual. However, wild stormy weather is not essential to sport in these months. A floating fly is the main requirement, and on a cold day it will work the greatest execution. Duns seem to prefer rather rigorous conditions, in summer at any rate, and in spring they have little objection to them, but for some reason or other fly-fishing has become associated with balmy breezes and sunny skies; perhaps it is because these duns seem fragile creatures. In July give me a cold day and an upstream breeze, the hatch is sure to come and the basket will be good.

13. J Colquhoun 1888
Worming for salmon

B ut the river salmon-fisher is more indebted to bait than either parr or minnow; and for this reason, that salmon will take a worm when the river is so low that they refuse all other kinds of prey. In river-angling a large hook should be used, and a mixture of dew-worms and the small red, or the brandling if it can be procured. The bait should be massy, nearly as thick as your little finger. This is accomplished by pushing up all the odds and ends of the worms you put on, along the shank of the hook and the gut, more or less, according to the angler's fancy. In rapid running water, a good lump of bait is more easily seen from a distance, and if a fresh worm be put on the point of the hook, the imposture cannot well be detected in the moving stream. Lead the line to reach within a yard or so of the bottom, and search every inch of pool and stream, noticing the slightest tug. When you perceive the least straightening of the line, always go over the same inch until you either fix the fish, or disgust him. Never be in a hurry with a large fish: give him time, if possible, to gorge. A good hold is half the battle with a good salmon, as, in a long-continued struggle, an indifferent one is apt to wear and give way, often at the few last faint efforts to spurn the shore.

Behind large stones and in eddies there is always a good cast for worm; and in searching the latter you cannot be too particular. Try every variety of depth and current; in fact, seem to humour the line, though dexterously guiding it.

14. J Colquhoun 1888
Mending a broken top

The following make-shift is inserted for the benefit of the luckless wight who may have the misfortune to break the top of his rod at the water-side, and neglected to bring a spare one. On the morning of my last day's fishing of the Echaig, I hooked a four-pound sea-trout on my bob, and when the fish was quite spent, the trail-fly fastened on a rotten stump. I waded in to try to disengage it, and, in so doing, carelessly strained back my rod over my right shoulder. The fish gave a languid plunge, and, of course, broke the top. Although I had only some thread, and a pair of scissors, I cut a couple of twigs, and spliced my rod, as clumsily as ever a country surgeon bungled a poor man's leg. With my maimed instrument I killed two fine salmon and several sea-trout. I had fished since July, and bagged two hundred and fifty-seven sea-trout, many very large, and twelve salmon and grilse, with the same top, and little expected to break it the last day, when I was particularly anxious to do great things. A few years ago, the same mishap befell me when fishing in Loch Drunkie. At the beginning of the day, a large yellow trout rose, and was fixed, just under a perpendicular bank. Not being able to land the fish without throwing back my rod too far, I snapped the top, though I secured my prey. Nothing daunted, I mended my rod with a bit of twine, and killed five more fine trout. I question if, either day, I should have had better sport had no accident occurred.

15. J Colquhoun 1888
Casting and working a salmon fly

I t is only in a stream of considerable bounds that the eminent
angler can fully display his power. Those brawling brooks
where salmon and grilse only ascend during floods, and
which can be commanded by a grilse-rod, are too much akin
to trouting to suit his taste. Such being, I will venture to say, the
feeling of all our leading salmon-anglers, it follows that to
command much water is a primary requisite. To give more power
in this respect, I have for many years adopted the plan of what is
called spinning the line. This consists in slowly pulling it through
the rings with the left hand, at the same time you are playing the
hook on the water. The advantages consist, first, in the more
enticing movements of the fly; next, in the greater command you
have of the tackle, should a fish rise; lastly, by enabling you to take
fuller and freer casts, especially when trees or other obstacles are
behind. Although not properly spinning, yet the line is pulled in
exactly like underhand trolling; with this difference, that in bait-
trolling the whole line is drawn through the rings (except the yard
at the rod-point with the appended bait), and lies coiled on the
bank, preparatory to the next throw; whereas in salmon-fishing
you can only draw in line until it touches the ground. By also
giving one or two turns of the line round the hand, there are about
two yards and a half saved from the back cast, and added to the
clean sweep of the river. Considerable knack is required; but when
a man is quite master of the cast, the line is delivered straight as a
rule, and the fly lights soft and smooth at the end of it. Having
thus fished with a long line to the foot of the pool or stream, most
anglers would wind up, and proceed to new water. I am loath to
do so (unless stinted by time), without giving the most likely spots
another chance by winding over them. This is done by fishing
backwards; – not *up* stream though – that would never do. Throw

the line fairly over the water you expect a fish to lie in, then wind up *very slowly* over him; continue taking a step or two backwards, repeating your long throw and slow wind over these choice places until you are satisfied.

16. J Colquhoun 1888
Trout taking a small black fly

T here is often in summer a small black fly that keeps playing on the top of the water, and every now and then alighting for a moment, as if tempting its aquatic foe. When the angler sees this fly thus sporting with the jaws of death, let him always have a small black hackle on his cast. There is also another summer-fly which comes down upon the river in great numbers, – they keep all together, and hover about two or three inches above the surface. The trout follow them in shoals, and in the Almond I have seen half-a-dozen heads at a time darting up at the busy throng above. As these flies do not alight on the water even for an instant, the trout are all intent on seizing them *in the air*, and there being generally a dead calm where these insects congregate, your cast, though thrown ever so lightly, has more the effect of alarming than of enticing the fish. It is most tantalising; but all that can be done is to take a few light casts now and then, *stopping whenever the trout cease to rise.* By this cautious proceeding, you may take one or two of the most greedy. When I have caught trout at such times, I have observed that they as often as not took the fly on the cast least resembling the insect.

17. J Colquhoun 1888
Worming for sea-trout

I once in this way astonished a fellow-craftsman, no mean performer either. I was at the burn-side just at the proper moment, and having fished the best of the water, was about to return after killing a couple of fine sea-trout, when I saw a rival, with whom I was unacquainted, trotting down to the bank. His first salutation was, 'Are the fish rising?' He then desired to see my flies, being a stranger to the burn. As he seemed what is called '*a greedy angler,*' I thought it no harm to take a *rise* out of *him*. The water by this time was long past its best; so, after supplying him with a fly, I said I would not interfere, but walk down and show him the casts. He was evidently a good fisher, but, as I anticipated, did not kill a fish, and only rose one. In the burn there was one very strong eddy, where the trout never rose to the fly, but where I seldom missed taking one with the worm, when the water was at all swollen. On coming near this place I said, if he had done nothing it was not his fault, but that I would now try my luck. I then let him go a good way ahead, took off my flies, put on a baithook and worm, and from this place pulled out two whitlings half-a-pound weight. I then whipped on my flies again, and overtook him at the end of the burn. I could hardly keep my gravity at his astonished face when I showed him my success. He never suspected the bait; and I soon took my leave, wishing him better sport the next spate!

18. J Colquhoun 1888
A salmon from Loch Slam

Lochs Slam, Craggie, and Layghal are all connected by a pretty large moor-burn, so the salmo-ferox inhabits the three. It is very seldom any are taken in Loch Slam, and only now and then in Loch Craggie; while Loch Layghal, from its greater size, is their chosen home. Loch Slam, however, has the first run of the salmon after a flood of the Borgie, and for a day or two there is a fine chance of hooking one, but they soon find the burn flowing out of Loch Craggie, when they all penetrate into that loch. Unless, therefore, you are so fortunate as to hit on the shoal on their first rush up the river into the loch from the sea, you may not stir a fish. I had once the good hap to light on these fresh-run salmon, and rose three – fixing one, which (as I had only good trouting single gut, and dared not check him) twice ran out two-thirds of my 100 yards reel-line. The sight of him rolling on the top of the water at such long distance certainly tried the nerves! His strength failed after these boring bursts, and I soon had him under command of a short line, when he played beautifully. He was a lovely-shaped salmon of 11½ lb, with the sea-lice on him.

19. J Colquhoun 1888
A ferox from Loch Loyal

The salmo-feroxes of these three lochs are scarcely equal to those of Loch Assynt at the other end of the county; while the Loch Shin trout taken by the troll are decidedly inferior to all these lochs – on which account I never took the trouble to fish it. The biggest ferox captured by us on Loch Layghal was secured by the worst-baited hook we ever insulted them with. Having used up all the best live bait, there only remained one or two small things quite unfit for trolling. I had landed at the Shepherd's brook for a fresh supply, while my son put on a couple of these tiny trout with scarcely an attempt to make them spin. Very soon this large ferox dashed at the clumsy lure, and, after a wicked struggle, was persuaded into the landing-net, and proved a large-headed, ill-shaped monster of 14 lb.

20. J D Dougall 1841
Twelve golden rules

1. Do not set a day on which to angle, as it may prove unfit for your sport, but have all your tackle in readiness, and start after a wet night, when the wind is westerly.

2. On reaching the river, first look at the state of the water, and see whether fly or bait is the more likely to be successful. If a loch, see whether the surface is much ruffled or not, and put on large or small flies accordingly.

3. Put up your rod and affix your tackle in a careful and secure manner. Never hurry.

4. If there are more than one in the party, fish pool about fairly and honestly. Three make the most pleasant party in angling.

5. If the rod of a companion breaks, help him to mend it; but if he calls out every half hour for assistance in mere trifles, as is the practice of many, refuse your aid.

6. If you angle in a strange water, and know not the best flies, always begin with a lark wing and haresear body, a woodcock wing and black hackle, and a teal wing and red hackle. You must have confidence in your flies: if you shift them too often you will lose much valuable time.

7. In spring, use dark-brown flies; in summer, small yellowish or jet-black flies; in autumn, larger and gaudier flies. The best months are March, April, July, August and September. Salmon fishing opens in the west of Scotland on the first day of February, and closes on the fourteenth of September. It is open much later on the Tweed.

8. If a churlish fellow refuses to show you his flies, hook them with your own, and generously offer to disengage them.

9. If you come in an excursion to a river that is preserved, go at once to the proprietor, and ask permission to fish, in a polite and respectful manner, and twenty to one you get it.

10. When you hook a fish, put him in your creel as quickly as possible: never trifle with any fish, or allow him to run out your line if you can prevent it. Keep the head of a large fish down the stream, *and keep opposite to him.*

11. Remember that time is everything: never idle it away while fishing, but fish every nook carefully and industriously. Try every thing. If they will not take the fly, try the worm. If they will not take the worm, try the minnow. Do not let yourself be beaten if industry will prevent it.

12. At the same time avoid all unfair modes of fishing, such as harrowing with the double rod, (except for salmon,) and using other instruments than the fair rod and line. If angling be a sport, it should be practised in a sportsmanlike manner.

21. A Dryden 1862
Angling near Edinburgh

T he Esk above Dalhousie is a good trouting stream. It divides into two branches. The one on the right is the Roseberry; the other is Temple Burn. One day I killed in the Esk thirteen dozen of trout which weighed 23 pounds. The Water of Leith is a good stream above Balerno Bridge. Four dozen and a half trout taken in this water weigh on an average 14 pounds. The Almond, which is the next tributary of the Firth of Forth, is the most difficult water from which to take trout that I ever fished in. But the trout are of excellent quality. They seem to be of the same nature as those found in lochs. They do not lie still watching for food, but keep always moving; so that after taking a fly, you will probably find that the fish has moved some yards before he takes another. Minnow is a good lure in the Almond. The trout average 4 to the pound; but through the whole river, you may kill them upwards of a pound in weight. Below the new bridge, eight miles from Edinburgh, the trout are heavier than they are higher up. You have the best chance of being successful in a wet day. There are several tributaries of the Almond which contain trout nearly as large as those which are to be found in the main stream; but they are not equal in other respects to those of the Almond. The first is the Gogar. The next is the Broxburn, good in the autumnal months. Then comes the Linn-house, which joins the Almond about Midcalder. This is the best of the tributaries. About 200 yards higher up, the Harburn joins the Linn-house. It is also a good stream.

The Avon falls into the Forth above Linlithgow. This was formerly a good trouting stream, but it has been utterly spoilt by chemical works. The Carron is a good stream a few miles from its mouth. Below the village of Denny the trout are scarce, but there are good skellies or chub to be got. A little above Denny there is good trout fishing, but the best of this water is for about a mile and a half both above and below Old Carron Bridge. There is the best water for May fly and creeper that I have had any experience of, and the bait is easily found by the river. There is also good artificial fly-fishing at the same place; for though the water is rather rough, there are many pools full of good trout. Higher up, is the Carron Fog. It is much too still for fishing, but further up you will come to a good little stream. In the Bannockburn I have killed good basketsful of trout, but, on the whole, I cannot say much in its praise. We now come to the Devon, running into the Forth on the north side, a little above Alloa. There are few rivers in the south of Scotland which can be compared with the Devon as a trouting stream. The size and quality of the trout are both good. The best are to be found below the village of Tillicoultry; but at certain seasons they are not easily caught, owing to the stillness of the water. I should say that the best part of the Devon is from Dollar upwards, but a good basketful may be taken between Tillicoultry and Dollar. The average size in the upper water is six to the pound. The Allan, on the same side of the Forth, affords fair fly-fishing from the Bridge of Allan up to Kemback, a distance of six miles. But the river runs roughly, and its bed consists of rocks and large stones, which make fishing in it unpleasant. The Allan has no tributaries worth mentioning, except the Knaik, falling in above Ardoch Bridge. In the Allan and its tributaries the trout vary very much in size. During the summer months, you will find in them both salmon, grilse, and sea trout, and the fishing is open to the public.

The Teith is the next tributary of the Forth. I need say little about it, as it is mostly preserved, and little worth preserving. There are large trout in it, but they are not numerous, and it is difficult to catch them. It is also infested with par. The Keltie runs into the Teith a little below Callander. The two streams are of similar character. Minnow is the best lure, or, if minnows cannot be got, par tail. But par tail I consider at all times an inferior bait to a minnow.

The Forth itself is one of the worst rivers for fishing in that I ever tried. It runs deep and black, and the trout are scarce; but it abounds in pike. Of the Earn in Perthshire I cannot say much in praise as a stream for common trout, but it is well stocked with perch, and sea trout are numerous. These vary in weight from one pound to two and a half. It is not difficult to take them when the river is a little swelled. The small ordinary trout-flies I have always found better than the larger ones. The sea trout are often to be caught in apparently the most unlikely spots. When the water is heavy, you may kill them with worm.

22. F Fernie 1912
Superiority of dry-fly angling

It may then be claimed for dry-fly fishing:

(1) That it is effective in the very best time of the year, and on the most pleasant days.

(2) That it is far more interesting than wet-fly fishing. A dry-fly angler may be compared to a 'googly' bowler, who must learn to bowl 'bad' balls 'on purpose,' so a dry-fly fisher must learn to cast sometimes with a slack line; but the bowler knows before he delivers it which ball in the over is intended to get the batsman out. The wet-fly man, on the other hand, is like the fast good-length bowler, who pegs away all the afternoon over after over: any ball before he delivers it is as likely to get a wicket as any other.

This bowler may be unplayable on a difficult wicket, or early in the season, just as a wet-fly angler may catch his dozens; but on a hard plumb wicket on a hot sunny day the slow bowler is likely to be more successful, just as the dry fly will beat the wet fly in very clear water.

(3) That it kills on the average bigger fish. This is admitted by nearly all Border fishermen, and the reason is that the dry-fly angler fishes chiefly the pools and still water where the best fish generally are, especially when the streams are low; besides the fact that the dry fly deceives the fish better than a wet fly.

(4) The capture of fish with a dry fly is all through the result of applied skill, whereas the capture of fish with wet flies, and particularly the hooking of them, is often a fluke.

Border fishermen talk of fish collectively as '*they* are not taking,' '*they're* no doin',' whilst dry-fly fishermen speak rather of fish individually.

To be successful with either wet or dry fly requires considerable skill and knowledge, and one would not care to give an opinion as to which requires the greater skill.

There is another method of wet-fly fishing, which consists in using one or more flies and fishing up stream. It is very nearly akin to dry-fly fishing, but is perhaps more difficult than the dry-fly or the ordinary down-stream wet-fly method, because it is hard to tell when to strike. It is very fully described in 'The Practical Angler' by Mr Stewart, who from that book might almost be shown to have been a dry-fly fisher in theory. For example:

'The moment the flies alight . . . being the only one in which trout take the artificial fly for a live one.'

'The moment the fly alights, being the most deadly of the whole cast.'

Two examples showing his appreciation of the fly floating.

Mr Stewart is here speaking of the *angler's* lure 'alighting' on the water. It is not necessary to suppose, as some have done, that he thought all the flies that fish feed on alight on the water, instead of rising from the bottom of the river, as, of course, the greater number do.

'To make the flies light in a soft and natural manner.'

'Take care that neither they [flies] nor the line ripple the surface.'

'The angler must endeavour to keep his line out of the main current, or his flies will come down too fast.'

Two examples of Mr Stewart's appreciation of 'drag' (*see* chap. ii).

'To throw them with certainty to any spot desired.'

23. F Fernie 1912
Feeding habits of trout

T rout in lochs are generally more fickle in their rising habits than in rivers; they mostly inhabit the shallower parts near shore, where the chief supply of food is. Probably larvæ and creatures that trout feed on do not inhabit very deep water; thus shallow lochs like Loch Leven will support a far greater weight of trout than deeper lochs of a similar area; and in general, shallow lochs contain a larger average size of trout, the difference lying in the food supply. The food of trout in lochs is much the same as in rivers, except that, I think, there are in a loch fewer varieties of flies. The principal kinds I have found are Olive Duns and Spinners, Caddis-flies and Black Gnats. Mr Malloch says the Loch Leven trout feed on Blood-worms, which Ronalds says are the larvæ of the Golden Dun.

It is difficult to know what the trout take the usual artificial loch flies for, but perhaps when feeding they are accustomed to take all kinds of flies, and take artificial flies the more readily because of their unfamiliar appearance. The theory of adjusting the size of the fly to the state of the water probably amounts to this: that in rough water a large fly is necessary to enable the fish to see it at all, and that in smooth water the fly must be small to prevent the fish from detecting its artificial nature. Mr P D Malloch ('Life-History of the Salmon,' &c.) says that loch trout travel about when feeding, usually against the wind, and that in Loch Leven the fish go at the rate of two to three miles per hour. Fish in lochs, however, do not always feed in this way. Many of them (at any rate in some lochs) take up permanent summer quarters just as they do in a river. I have often seen the same fish rise within an area of about one square yard over and over again, and evening after evening. I have frequently put down a fish in a certain place and come back, half an hour afterwards, to find him rising again. There are lots of places in lochs where there are big stones and rocks on the bottom, where one may rise fish every day; but fifty yards away on either side one never gets a rise. There is one place on Loch Tay, over a little submerged island, where fish are often feeding, but as soon as one gets off it not a rise can be had. Surely in such places the fish have taken up a permanent residence, chiefly on account of the shelter afforded by the stones.

The fact that fish travel always against the wind may explain why on some lochs they can only be caught when the wind is in a particular direction, since it might be made possible by some effect of light dependent on the particular surroundings of the loch; or perhaps the fish know from experience that food is only blown on the water when a certain wind is blowing. It is probable that in some lochs the fish *must* travel about in order to get sufficient food. They must also sometimes be travelling (although perhaps not feeding) *with* the wind, otherwise they would in a short time be all congregated at one end of the loch.

24. F Fernie 1912
Places to fish on Tweed and Clyde waters

Peebles is a good centre from which to fish the Tweed, and here, as is now the practice on most Border streams, a local Angling Association keeps watchers, and issues angling tickets at a small charge. This policy is likely to do an immense amount of good to the fishing, which was rapidly being ruined by netting. It is possible that in the near future one big association may get powers to control all the trout fishing in the South of Scotland; but the best of all remedies for poaching would be to make the exposure of trout for sale illegal. At present, on some of the streams, water that is nominally private is netted far more than water under the care of an angling association. The Jed, a very sporting stream, and parts of the Teviot have lately suffered cruelly from netting. A shocking ruffian whom I used to meet on a certain stretch of Teviot, and who was in the habit of smoking my tobacco, would often point out to me which pools had recently been netted! Roxburgh is a good centre for Teviot. Leader, an ideal trout stream, and Gala are conveniently fished from Lauder and Stow. Tickets for Leader can be obtained in Lauder and Earlston. No one should grudge paying the very modest charge made, since all the money is used for paying watchers to keep the nets off. Chirnside is a convenient place for the Whiteadder, another excellent stream. A man who fairly often fishes it told me he had hardly ever fished more than a length of about 200 yards, and there he finds enough sport for a whole day.

The Clyde is good near Biggar. I think the Tweed is rather understocked at present, but it will doubtless improve as its tributaries become better looked after. From 6 oz to 1 lb. is about the average weight, but occasionally fish of 4 lb. and 5 lb. are caught. In Yarrow and Leader the fly fisher should have no difficulty in getting three or four brace of ½ lb. trout on a good morning in June. On Teviot and Clyde the average weight of fish caught with a dry fly is well over ½ lb.

The English visitor need not have the slightest fear of being crowded on any of the open water. Except on Saturday afternoons and public holidays, and in the evenings near a town, it is rarely that more than one or two anglers are met with during a whole day; and I can recall days on Tweed, Teviot, Ettrick, Yarrow, Leader, and Gala on which I have never met any one else fishing at all.

Nowhere can the angler find cheaper fishing than is to be had in the Border district. Comfortable quarters at a reasonable price, either at an inn or in a cottage, can be found everywhere, amongst a most kindly, hospitable, tactful people, innately well bred, who form a great contrast to those in some other parts of the country, where one can hardly ask the way without paying a shilling for the information.

25. F Francis 1874
The Stanley water on the Tay

I n the afternoon we drove out to the Stanley water, which is
some seven or eight miles from Perth. This water is classical and
world-renowned, for it was here that Leech derived his
inspiration for the cartoons of old Briggs catching that historical
salmon. Here is the 'Cat hole' where he hooked his salmon, and
there that tremendous run he took him down – and a very nasty run
it is! and there, too, is Hell hole, where the redoubtable salmon
sulked! and that, as I live, is an exact sketch of the very spot where
that wonderful gillie is taking his 'sneesh!' and here Mr Briggs landed
the fish clasped in his embrace; and there is the very boat, too, in
which he sat beaming upon the river, with the three rods spread out
before him! Who could fail to recognise the scene where befell the
greatest event in Mr Briggs's sporting career? It is splendid water that
Stanley water – such a succession of rattling, rapid streams and swirls,
that I doubt if there be so fine a bit elsewhere on the Tay. It was too
early for any chance of moving a fish, so we had walked on up the
river to inspect the water. Above the Stanley water comes the
Burnmouth water – a fine, long, open pool, for a considerable
portion of it, which always holds fish, and that too of the largest.
At the top of the Burnmouth water is the Linn of Campsie, where the
rocky shores approach each other very closely indeed, and, with the
exception of an insignificant side stream, the whole of the Tay here
pours in a resistless volume through a narrow neck not much more
than twenty yards wide, into a deep, dark, foam-flecked swirling pool
below, which resembles a huge basin. A fine view of the Linn is
obtained from the high rocks which overhang the north side. Here
formerly a monastery stood, and faint traces are still to be seen of its
walls. The scenery is very fine, and is alone worth a visit. Having seen
all that we cared to see, we scrambled through the woods, over the
cliffs, where a slip or a fall in places would drop one into the river, one
hundred feet or more below, back to the Stanley water. The boat was
ready for us, and embarking with two rods, each with a brace of flies

BY LAKE AND RIVER:

AN

ANGLER'S RAMBLES

IN THE

NORTH OF ENGLAND AND SCOTLAND.

BY FRANCIS FRANCIS.

Author of " A Book on Angling," &c., &c.

LONDON :
"THE FIELD" OFFICE, 346, STRAND.
1874.

on, and one with a phantom minnow, we commenced the usual see-saw to and fro. A good many fish were rising and showing themselves. They were kelts, old red winter fish, and a few clean fish – but not one would even make an offer at us; and after about a couple of hours assiduous hurling without any result, we gave it up, got back to our trap, and so home, It was clear that, barring the accident of a dark and windy day – which seemed to avoid us as much as possible – fishing in the Tay was hopeless. It was also full late for spring-fishing, and too early for grilse.

26. F Francis 1874
Angling in Loch Awe

T he next day we left, and returned to the Clyde. I know no
pleasanter spot to spend a fortnight in, wind and weather
permitting, than Loch Awe. If the rambler be a keen fisher,
there he may indulge to his heart's content either in fly fishing or
trolling. In the first he will, judging by the list of takes of past years
shown in the book kept at the inn, pick up from one dozen to two
and a half dozens of good trout to his own rod, which will average
half a pound. Now, when I say this I mean honest *weighed* weight. If
I were speaking loosely by ordinary fisherman's estimate, I should
certainly say they averaged three-quarters, and that several of the fish
would run over a pound; but Cameron won't let you guess weights,
he scales the fish to an ounce, and as it is they run nearly a pound,
which is all the difference. But these Loch Awe fish are among the
gamest I ever handled, and for their size are tough antagonists; they
jump out of water, and scurry hither and thither, with an agility that
keeps the angler in pleasant excitement, and a pound fish is a strong
fighter who will take ten minutes to kill. They are capital eating, cut
red and firm, and mighty good for breakfast. Now and then you will
take a sea trout or two – I got hold of two one day, but the largest
was only some three-quarters of a pound.

For fly fishing, May and early June are the best season. Trolling
certainly is not as hopeless a case as it is on some lochs I could
mention, only one never sticks at it when the fish are rising; and, as
that is the time when they would also be running it is mostly pursued
at the most unfavourable and unlikely times, and is therefore not so
successful as it might be. But, though the ferox is not nearly as
plentiful as formerly in Loch Awe, there are still a good few in the
lake, and a bottle of preserved dace would, I am sure, answer well
here. The practice now is to use artificial baits – the Angel, the
Phantom, &c.; and, excellent as the Phantom is, and it is universally
used in all this part of Scotland, still it cannot equal the natural bait,
which many fish, I am sure, might be killed with. The ferox do not as

a rule run large – under 6 lb. I should say – but every now and then a thumper makes his appearance; one of 17 lb. was taken a day or two after I left, as I heard. Ferox are generally indifferent eating, but the 2½ lb. fish mentioned above was by no means a bad fish. We had him boiled for dinner, and the head and tail alone were left when we had done with it. I stole the jaw, however, to bring it home for comparison, and then, like a fisherman (I was going to say something else), I forgot to compare it. There are a few salmon in the lake, as well as sea trout; but the throws are not well known, or the fish are capricious, and the lake is very large, so that it is more often an accident than not when one is hooked. If the angler likes to go in for pike and perch, unfortunately in some bays there are plenty. The perch often run large, but I never happened to get hold of a pike, though I trolled a good deal at times, which rather surprised me. Still, I must believe that there are plenty; for if they once got into the lake, they couldn't fail to increase. Formerly they were kept down a good deal by set nets; but no one seems to have any interest in doing so now, and the lake, which had greatly improved under this regimen, is now, I am told, going back again under its abandonment. Surely the innkeepers might do something, if the proprietors are supine. Mr Malcolm, who is a very large proprietor on the lake side, and is also a sportsman, if he only gave the word to his keepers, might do much good. He is building a large hotel at Sonnachan, and, in the interest of the coming customers, he might at least help to keep the pike down.

27. A Grimble 1902
Good and bad salmon fisheries

I n writing of a good fishery, we mean one which shows a fine average for many years past, for it is impossible to insure a uniform good take, and all anglers will be able to recall cases of large rents being paid for fishings yielding next to nothing, though for many previous seasons the catch has been large and renowned. Our idea of a good fishery is that each rod on it should get from fifty to a hundred fish during the two months of the best season, and any piece of water showing this amount of sport before the middle of July is worth twice as much as one offering the like attractions in autumn.

In writing of a downright bad fishery, we mean one that has had ten fresh tenants in as many years, and in which the two best months have averaged fifteen fish a rod, while the rent asked has been from a hundred to two hundred pounds. Of this sort there are always some in the market, and nothing will ever deter rash anglers from taking them; so that it appears to be useless to repeat the worn-out caution of advising fishermen never to rent any water from which they cannot get a return of the sport had on it for several years.

28. A Grimble 1902
Playing a salmon

As to what is good time in which to kill a fish, it is an accepted law by many old hands that a pound a minute is smart work. It may be prolonged by a sulky fish; but with the rod in good hands, we hold such an event as a long sulk should not be permitted to happen, unless indeed it is impossible to get below the 'sulky brute', for on such occasions all fish at once become 'brutes'. We have never met with one that could resist, for more than a few minutes, the weight of a long line and a steady pull down stream from the middle of the rod. Out from behind the sulking place it must come, but look out for squalls, as a rush down stream may drown the line; but never mind if it does, and laugh even if the hold be broken, for anything is better than standing still, pulling steadily at a fish for an hour or so; it makes one feel and look like a fool. Therefore, do not be afraid to go even fifty or sixty yards below the sulker, all the while paying out line step by step, while keeping up a heavy strain, with the rod held low, and nearly parallel to the water. As the strain begins to tell, the fisherman will get warning of the impending move by feeling a tug or two as the captive endeavours to keep his place; as he gives way, then upright the rod and get in every inch of line possible. Go up to meet him, if he will let you, and try to get opposite him, a position which once attained should soon end the combat. At times a fish will sulk in such a position as renders it impracticable to get below him, and then indeed he is almost master of the situation. Costly messages may be sent him down the line in the shape of a valuable bunch of keys, which we once saw done, without producing the least effect; the gillie may throw any amount of stones, but when sulking occurs in deep, sluggish water, and there is no boat to be had so that the surly one can be poked out of his lair by oar or sting, and unless the angler has seen he is in an extraordinary large fish which it would be a glorious matter to take, then it is best to put on a severe strain for twenty minutes or so, gradually increasing it till either the fish moves or something breaks.

29. A Grimble 1902
Bait fishing for salmon

T o some bigoted anglers bait-fishing is a detestable method of catching salmon, so much so that by the very rabid ones this has been described as equivalent to shooting a hare on its form. Well, if it was *really impossible* to kill a hare running, then, we confess, if we were hare-shooting and wanted one badly, we would certainly kill it sitting. There are many reaches of water through which spring fish run without a halt, while as they will not take a fly when travelling, and yet will take a bait, we consider that fact to be a very good reason for using one. Admitting we would rather catch a fish with a fly than by any other lure, we own to being so constituted that to come home blank is the abomination of desolation. To work hard at anything the whole day long for nothing does not suit our temperament, for after such an event, dinner is not enjoyed, sleep fails us, breakfast next morning is hateful, and peace of mind can only again be restored by a tight line. In sport, as in all other matters, live and let live has ever been our motto; without going the length of some bait-fishers, who call the fly an antiquated old lure, we do not hesitate to resort to bait of every sort, if by so doing a duck's egg for the day is saved. No one who dislikes bait-fishing need practise it, while those who object to it are usually fishermen having some of the picked fishings of a river, in which the salmon will lie for weeks, and if they will not rise one day they will be sure to do so on another.

30. E Hamilton 1884
Playing a salmon

When a salmon, being hooked, after a minute or so begins jobbing and shaking your line – a most unpleasant feeling, which sends a kind of nervous dread through you – nine cases out of ten on examination it is found that he is hooked in the upper jaw, leaving his gills full play, and so he is able by this manœuvre sometimes to lose the hold, or break the hook if in the bone, but often it does the contrary – it tightens the hold. The most killing place (when the hook is well fast) is in the lower jaw. The strain of the line prevents in a great measure the free current of water through the gills, and the fish becomes suffocated; a curious instance of this occurred to a friend with whom I was fishing. He hooked a fresh-run salmon of 16 lb., and to his astonishment, after a rapid whirl of the reel, and a fight of five minutes, the fish came up on his side and was soon on the bank. He found the hook had gone into both jaws, thus entirely closing the mouth and suffocating the fish. Something of the same kind occurred to myself. I had hooked a good fish, had a fearful fight to prevent him getting under some snags lying deep at the upper part of the pool, and in the last struggle, when he was well beat, in keeping him on the top of the water, I nearly lost him from his pertinacity to get down to where he knew he could break me, and I had to gaff him in a very ticklish place. After killing him I threw again in the same place; up came another fish, and he followed the same tactics, when suddenly he came up on his side completely beat. I found in his struggle he had by some means got the line round his mouth, so that he was suffocated.

That delightful author and excellent fly fisher, Theophilus South, says: – 'I never strain a fish except he approaches dangerous ground,' and excellent advice it is. Many a good fish is lost by straining him unnecessarily, or in other words, giving him the butt too soon. The *suaviter in modo* and *fortiter in re* is the right motto in salmon fishing – to know when to put the strain on. Some years ago I hooked a good fish in the Ness in the run above the 'Twa Stanes' Pool. After

RECOLLECTIONS

OF

FLY FISHING

FOR

SALMON, TROUT, AND GRAYLING,

WITH NOTES ON

THEIR HAUNTS, HABITS, AND HISTORY.

BY

EDWARD HAMILTON, M.D., F.L.S., &c.

ILLUSTRATED BY A MEZZOTINT ENGRAVING BY FRANCIS SEYMOUR HADEN, ESQ., AND FIVE FULL PAGE WOOD ENGRAVINGS FROM SKETCHES BY THE AUTHOR.

Second Edition.

LONDON:

SAMPSON LOW, MARSTON, AND CO., LIMITED,

St. Dunstan's House,

FETTER LANE, FLEET STREET, E.C.

1891.

(All rights reserved.)

two or three minutes he went up stream with the speed of lightning, running out 100 yards of my line. I had only 110 on the reel. Mackenzie, my gillie, was in an awful pucker. 'Oh, give him the butt, sir! – stop him! – he will break you! – hold up your rod! Oh dear, what a grand fish!' We were running like mad all this time. If I had moved my rod he must have broke me in an instant. I felt this and was as steady as possible; suddenly he stopped. During the whole course of my fishing experience I have never seen a fish run like this one. The force and rapidity were so great that the rod was fairly bent down. After a quarter of an hour away he went again down as far as the Twa Stanes, when he suddenly turned up again, but then I put the strain on him, and turned him; down he came again, passed the Twa Stanes, into the pool below and right across it. 'He must not go there, we can't follow him if he does,' said Mackenzie; so then the butt was given with a vengeance, and what a pleasant feeling came over me when I found he yielded, and we soon brought him to bank, a fine fresh-run fish of 21½ lb., and the sea-louse upon him.

31. E Hamilton 1884
Salmon fly patterns

Whenen one sees the gaudy paraphernalia in the fishing-tackle makers' shops, one's heart sinks, but I suppose they must be of some use. It would be interesting if we could get a record of the results of the well-known flies, the Pophams, the Butchers, the Doctors, etc., etc., as to their killing powers, – something in the same manner as Mr W. Balderson has done with the trout flies, as lately given in 'The Fishing Gazette.'

My experience in salmon fishing has been principally in the autumn months, August, September, and October, and with the exception of the Blue or Silver Doctor and the Jock Scott, and occasionally the Sun fly, I always use sober-coloured flies, with excellent results. There are four especial patterns which I never am without; the Western Butcher, a very different fly to the gaudy gentleman we find in the shops (but he also is a capital fly at times), dressed on two different sized hooks, Nos. 6 and 9, Limerick Body of dark maroon mohair, silver twist; wings, grouse feather with two strands of blue macaw; hackle, jay's wing mixed with some few dark strands; tail, golden pheasant hackle.

The Harriet. – Body, purple mohair, silver twist; wings, turkey; hackle, blue jay; tail, golden pheasant. No. 5 and No. 8 hooks. A deadly fly when fish are in the humour.

The August Brown. – Body, light brown mohair, gold twist; wings of the gled tail or bittern; hackle, dark brown. Nos. 5 and 8 hooks. A first-rate fly in full water dressed on No. 5.

The Black Doctor. – Body, black mohair, silver twist; wings, grouse feather; hackle, a few strands of blue jay and black; tail, yellow strands of golden pheasant; also without the tail. A splendid fly dressed on two-sized hooks, Nos. 6 and 9.

The later in the autumn the smaller should be the flies.

However, as all fishermen know, the fish must be in the humour, and this so much depends on circumstances over which we have no control. There is one thing, however, worth observing, viz., the

barometer. I have often found that fish will not sport with a falling barometer, however well the day may look or however softly or favourably the wind may blow. Still this is not always so; fish are curious customers, and there is no accounting for their vagaries.

I usually have my flies dressed on two sized hooks, and I prefer the double hook, it is not more clumsy and gives a better chance of a kill. Here is a good instance: –

I was fishing on the Spean, and after a very provoking day, the fish rising and just touching the fly, towards evening I got hold of a good fish. He kept shaking his head very persistently, and I felt the hook was not well fixed: however, I landed him, just over twenty pounds, and found he was hooked in the upper jaw. He had managed to get rid of one hook, and there was the laceration caused by it in the mouth, but fortunately the other held. Had I been fishing with a single hook, considering the way the fish had been rising all day, I probably should have lost him.

32. J A Harvie-Brown 1898
Up-stream casting analysed

T he one counted the other's casts, timing with a stop-watch, and repeated the experiment over and over again to test its accuracy. The conclusion was arrived at that the one who was angling made fifteen casts in one minute. He who was fishing thus was not at the time aware of the presence behind him of his friend. Therefore if a day's fishing be put down at, say, six hours (we are usually content with much less), fifteen a minute would give 5400 casts per diem. By deducting one hour for lunch and other intervals – 'fankles,' pipes, and landing and netting one's fish – that figure would be reduced to 4500 casts. As Stewart tells us, the alighting of the fly is the most deadly in the whole cast, therefore the oftener it is repeated the better. Later on, when we intend to speak of the actual process and practice, and describe the fishing-up of a reach or pool or stream, we may make the reason of such frequent casting more distinct. Meanwhile let us ask the question: How many casts will the down-stream fisher make per hour, or per minute, when covering four miles of bank and acres of water with his line. We leave the question to be answered by the 'down-streamer.' The hard work in 'down-streaming' comes in, not for the arms, and eyes, and mind, but in the cubits, and the strides, and mileage, and weight of the pole.

It is seldom needful to use a longer line than one and a half times the length of the rod – *i.e. if wading up*; nor a longer rod than a single-handed twelve-foot rod. Yet we have seen otherwise good up-stream anglers using too long a line, which ought to become evident to themselves, if they observed the continuous loss of time by 'fankling' and subsequent mismanagement at the time of a rise of fish – all hurry and little speed, curses not loud but deep, and sometimes accompanied by frantic gestures. 'The nearer we are to our flies the better we can use them, and the greater the chance of hooking'.

33. J A Harvie-Brown 1898
Vision and behaviour of trout

I t appears to us to be a mere begging of the question to use as an argument that the colour of insects, as seen by us, is comparable with what may be seen by fish. Fish see through a different medium from ours, and surely we see differently through theirs. Or does Stewart mean to uphold that they see similarly through their medium with us through ours? We must continue to look upon colours, to the eye of a fish, as an unknown quality. One fact however is, if nothing else, suggestive. Many times, when trying an underhand cast to get the tail-fly over a rising fish, under an alder or a broken down reed, has our fly been hung up, and the tail-fly has been suspended some four to six inches over his 'wonderful snout,' and we have seen trout or trouts spring clear out of water and hook on to that fly, and, as you may suppose, 'generally stuck to it too.' This proves they can see through both media of water and air. The other illustration we like to repeat, viz. the 'man of cubits and the pole,' whose common colour is black! A 'black hackle' is equally a killer on a bright summer day and on a dark moonless night. It is the most killing fly for instance, on Loch Earn, for both trout and char, when it is too dark for the angler to see his line or flies. This proves they can see as *we can not*. But a white fly – a 'coachman' also kills well on a dark night. Hence arises another phase of the inquiry: Do trout rise best because they see too well, or because they only see movement under differently coloured waters or skies?

34. J A Harvie-Brown 1898
Always up-stream for trout

A n advocate of down-stream fishing once stated in our
hearing, if not indeed in black and white, 'If it were not
that the up-stream angler selected his spots, he would have
no chance with the down-streamer.' To this we reply, 'We prefer
trout-angling to salmon-fishing for trout,' and the beauty of fishing
up appears to us to be the knowledge acquired and the natural
selection which follows such education.

Many, indeed most, anglers prefer to fish down, when heavy
down-stream winds render it too difficult and too fatiguing to fish
up; and, indeed, in such weather there are many days in which the
up-stream casts are made almost impossible. But Stewart advocates
the attempt even then. It is possible at times to fight the wind across
by a peculiar underhand flick, difficult to describe and not always easy
to attain to, sending out the line on the same plane with the surface
of the water; but this requires a stiff rod, and cannot be said to be very
satisfactory. Another plan is to cover a larger mileage of water, and
thereon select only such bends or reaches as are negotiable. We have
taken many a fair basket in this way under adverse circumstances. A
third way – and where neither of the above are found to be
practicable – is to take Stewart's advice as conveyed on pp. 117–
118, and 'you will be more able to fish properly' another time.

An angler friend of experience writes: – 'Yes; I have no doubt
whatever, from experience, that the underhand cast is the best plan
"under," the wind.' We have said it is difficult to describe, as well as
not always easy to do, but perhaps the following may convey the idea:
– The action is somewhat similar to that of a round-hand bowler,
when he attempts to put a 'break back' upon the ball at the pitch.
And in angling, and attempting to dodge a flaw of wind, the same
motion, as when he tries to 'put on a twist' from leg in cricket. But in
angling the whole action is not an entire arm-action, but should be
done by forearm and wrist only.

145

THE
WONDERFUL TROUT

BY

J. A. HARVIE-BROWN

'*Thus does the salmon vault.*'
DRYDEN.

EDINBURGH : DAVID DOUGLAS

10 CASTLE STREET

1898

35. J A Harvie-Brown 1898
Baits and illegal methods for trout

A mongst other devices for capturing trout, we merely desire to mention them by name, adding a few remarks here and there.

Green worm in a yellow flood. – Many may think we have said enough or too much already.

Salmon roe is illegal. I done it 'wanst,' but it was not in midsummer!

Snatching is illegal, for salmon. I never done it; but the acts don't work. *The Black Watch-it insec'* often looking on helpless.

Guddling, or 'gunnling,' or 'tickling.' I have. Good fun for a boy, but illegal.

Ottering. – I have done or seen it done twice. Don't see any fun in it. 'Rives' and tears, and renders shy scores of pricked fish. Illegal, but commonly practised in spite of the law.

Cross-lining. – Illegal and destructive. Never did it, but have seen it done, for both salmon and trout, by a laird and his keeper. (*Game*keeper, I mean.)

Fishing with twelve flies on a cast. – Clyde only, I believe; *open* water (very)!

Set lines. – Done it – *for eels* or monsters. Never caught many of the latter. Only a few, when one wanted to 'give a loch a fair chance,' when it was 'outwith jurisdiction'; but went on the same principle as the Quaker who said, 'Thou may do it this time, friend, but thou mayst not make a practice thereof.'

Netting. – Have done it once, by permission, to try and reduce an unnecessary stock of small trout in a Highland loch. Party: three 'sportsmen,' six gillies, a pony, and a 'lassie' looking after the pony. Result: one small trout to each, some boulders, more mud, and a ducking. Didn't try it again!

'*Burning the Watter.*' – Done it twice: fell out of the boat, got nasty and wet, but thought it grand fun, though not *sport*!

Dynamite. – Saw it done in a Hungarian river once. Disgusting! Never desire to see it any more. Dastardly!

Night-fishing. – Done it often. Not keen on it. Cause of bad language.

Blue-bottle fly. – Used to practise this and kill, but gave it up in maturer years.

Creeper. – Ditto.

Diving minnow. – Ditto, and rather liked it.

Par-tail and minnow. – There is a phase of this which *is* sport, *i.e.* up-stream fishing with minnow. I am not an adept at it, but can realise that it is 'sport.' No doubt minnow is legitimate 'sport,' and 'par-tail' is a good bait for getting rid of rubbish, *i.e.* old big trout, which are cannibals with big teeth and do more harm in a stream than good, and ought to be killed at all seasons, as I think so should old black cocks and even old grey hens and old cock grouse all the year round.

36. J Hicks 1855
Trouting in Loch Urigil

W e commenced fishing to-day at the south end, and proceeding along the western shore, performed the entire circuit of Loch Urigil, and good hard work we found it. The lake is about two miles in length, which, in addition to the rounding of its extremities, and a frequent circuit back from promontories, round bays, and (when on shore) a very fagging walk over peat moss, bogs, and rock, to say nothing of the exertion of fishing, and perpetual wading, amounts to a distance and labour, which will suffice most men requiring a day's exercise. We must not forget the road to and from the lake, which has already been described. In short, fishing round Loch Urigil, without a boat, is a business requiring health, strength, and endurance, and, perhaps what is more than equal to strength, a thorough love of the angler's employment, which feels neither cold, wet, nor fatigue.

There is a burn flowing out of Loch Urigil at the north end (which we had to wade nearly to our waists), in which I took five trout in six casts, averaging above half a pound each. The sum total of our captures to-day, amounted to two hundred and twelve. Early in the season, on a favourable day, we should, in all probability, have had thrice that number.

37. J Hicks 1855
A Highland boat at Altnacealgach

T his boat, not two years old, was never water-tight, the nails not being properly clinched, and a large hole in her bottom had never been properly repaired; the rude means adopted for stopping this aperture, consisted in the application of a piece of turf, above which a heavy stone was placed. Her increased leaking to-day, was caused by the loss of the original stone, and the substitution of one too light to resist the force of the water. We landed in a bay, where having stuffed the orifice with a fresh piece of turf and a heavier stone, we launched again, and continued fishing till the breeze subsided. I have mentioned the mode adopted of repairing this leaking boat, as an instance of the rude manner in which things are done in this remote district.

38. R Knox 1854
Biology of Loch Leven trout

T he angler, leaving Edinburgh, will find no difficulty in reaching Kinross; the lake is at hand; as it is private property, he must engage a boat from the tenant, and in it rowing to a small rocky island towards its northern shore, he lands at the foot of that ruined castle, once the prison of Marie Stuart.

Should the wind be strong and favourable, the angler may readily enough take some good trout, as I did. The fly used was a large one, like those we used on Prestmannan Lake. It was in autumn. The trout of Loch Leven taken with nets in great numbers, to be sent all over the kingdom, and at high prices, is a beautiful, silvery, dark-spotted trout, of a species quite distinct from all river trout, and imagined by some to be peculiar to the lake. This, however, is not likely, since trout quite resembling those of Leven are found in many northern lakes. The flesh is of a fine pink colour; the eating admirable. During summer and autumn, when examined (and I have opened hundreds to ascertain the fact), the trout has its stomach filled with flies and insects, the ordinary food of the common river trout; but, in addition, it is often found to have been living on a small buccinum, or fresh-water whelk, with which the shallow waters of the lake abound.

But the great peculiarity of the trout of Loch Leven is the fact that, in December, January, and February, many Loch Leven trout come into market, and are then found to be in the highest condition; at a time when river trout are everywhere out of season and unfit for food. Curious to discover the cause of this, I examined a very great number of these winter and early spring trout. In all, I found that the food they had been living on was microscopic; that is, entomostracan, so small that the microscope was required to make out distinctly the character of the food. These trout were in fact subsisting, thriving, and fattening on the food used by the char and the vengis, and by the herring. I am thus disposed to think that two species of trout inhabit Loch Leven, independent of the

151

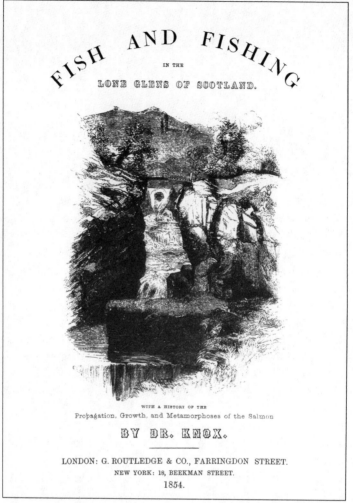

FISH AND FISHING

IN THE

LONE GLENS OF SCOTLAND.

WITH A HISTORY OF THE
Propagation, Growth, and Metamorphoses of the Salmon

BY DR. KNOX.

LONDON: G. ROUTLEDGE & CO., FARRINGDON STREET.
NEW YORK: 18, BEEKMAN STREET.
1854.

common river trout, namely, the trout which lives on entomostracæ, and comes into season in December, January, and February: and the trout, which feeding on the buccinum, and on flies, worms, and all the common food of the common river trout, comes into season much later in spring. If this view be the true one, then the early trout of Loch Leven ought to be called the char-trout, as being allied to the char in its habits and general character.

39. R Knox 1854
Coarse fish in Lochmaben and the Annan

Behold us now at Lochmaben, and close to the Annan and the Ae, both good trouting streams; but above all, as regards scenery, in the neighbourhood of that beautiful lake, the Castle Loch of Lochmaben; and on its shady banks the ruined Castle of 'the Brus.' Here, if we can trust history, lived one of the great Norman robbers, called Robert de Brus. He had other castles besides this one, for the original seat of the family was Guisborough, in Yorkshire; the Scotch estates came, I think, by marriage. The castle has a still stronger interest than even this, though Bannockburn will live long in story; this castle was one of the residences of Marie Stuart, queen of Scotland. The lake, which at one time had surrounded the castle by means of an artificial moat, contains fish of various kinds, but not many trout. Pike abound, but chief and foremost is the vengis or vendiss, thought to have been transplanted to this lake by the early monks. Of this curious and beautiful fish, a number of idle stories were told, until the rubbish was cleared away by myself; the most curious part of its history was, that it could not be tempted by any bait. Now this was true, and the cause thereof was demonstrated for the first time by myself. The vendiss live on minute microscopic entomostraca, a kind of shellfish, declining all other food.

Before I describe the vengis or vendiss, let me say a few words about angling in the Annan. It is not a particularly good river for this purpose, being much poached and scourged by the idle and profligate of the village. But it contains trout and parr, sea trout and hirling, salmon and bull trout in their season; besides pike and bream, and other coarse fish. The country around is primitive, and many originals live on its banks, and around the lakes of Lochmaben. The vendiss, shorn of its mystery, is still fished at a particular time of the year with nets, and ate in season – a kind of whitebait dinner for some old-fashioned people. It brings them together – suspends for an hour or two the little animosities which all farmers and small lairds have to their next neighbours – and benefits the inns. When other topics fail, they talk of Johnny Armstrong and the Border robbers. Abhorring clubs and whitebait dinners, I always avoided these vendiss clubs, but I have often eaten the vendiss when just from the lake. It is a moderately good fish to eat, but not to be compared to the Loch Leven trout. The professed naturalist arranges the vendiss with the family of the Corrigoni, a hard word to pronounce. Vendiss is better and softer, so is vengis, of whose root we know nothing. A fish of the same sort, but specifically different, is abundant enough in Loch Lomond. They occur also, though not of the same species, in Wales; in North America the natural family abounds.

40. A Lang 1895
Confessions of a duffer

These papers do not boast of great sport. They are truthful, not like the tales some fishers tell. They should appeal to many sympathies. There is no false modesty in the confidence with which I esteem myself a duffer, at fishing. Some men are born duffers; others, unlike persons of genius, become so by an infinite capacity for not taking pains. Others, again, among whom I would rank myself, combine both these elements of incompetence. Nature, that made me enthusiastically fond of fishing, gave me thumbs for fingers, short-sighted eyes, indolence, carelessness, and a temper which (usually sweet and angelic) is goaded to madness by the laws of matter and of gravitation. For example: when another man is caught up in a branch he disengages his fly; I jerk at it till something breaks. As for carelessness, in boyhood I fished, by preference, with doubtful gut and knots ill-tied; it made the risk greater, and increased the excitement if one did hook a trout. I can't keep a fly-book. I stuff the flies into my pockets at random, or stick them into the leaves of a novel, or bestow them in the lining of my hat or the case of my rods. Never, till 1890, in all my days did I possess a landing-net. If I can drag a fish up a bank, or over the gravel, well; if not, he goes on his way rejoicing. On the Test I thought it seemly to carry a landing-net. It had a hinge, and doubled up. I put the handle through a buttonhole of my coat: I saw a big fish rising, I put a dry fly over him; the idiot took it. Up stream he ran, then down stream, then he yielded to the rod and came near me. I tried to unship my landing-net from my button-hole. Vain labour! I twisted and turned the handle, it would not budge. Finally, I stooped, and attempted to ladle the trout out with the short net; but he broke the gut, and went. A landing-net is a tedious thing to carry, so is a creel, and a creel is, to me, a superfluity. There is never anything to put in it. If I do catch a trout, I lay him under a big stone, cover him with leaves, and never find him again. I often break my top joint; so, as I never carry string, I splice it with a bit of the line, which

I bite off, for I really cannot be troubled with scissors and I always lose my knife. When a phantom minnow sticks in my clothes, I snap the gut off, and put on another, so that when I reach home I look as if a shoal of fierce minnows had attacked me and hung on like leeches. When a boy, I was – once or twice – a bait-fisher, but I never carried worms in box or bag. I found them under big stones, or in the fields, wherever I had the luck. I never tie nor otherwise fasten the joints of my rod; they often slip out of the sockets and splash into the water. Mr Hardy, however, has invented a joint-fastening which never slips. On the other hand, by letting the joint rust, you may find it difficult to take down your rod. When I see a trout rising, I always cast so as to get hung up, and I frighten him as I disengage my hook. I invariably fall in and get half-drowned when I wade, there being an insufficiency of nails in the soles of my brogues. My waders let in water, too, and when I go out to fish I usually leave either my reel, or my flies, or my rod, at home. Perhaps no other man's average of lost flies in proportion to taken trout was ever so great as mine. I lose plenty, by striking furiously, after a series of short rises, and breaking the gut, with which the fish swims away. As to dressing a fly, one would sooner think of dressing a dinner. The result of the fly-dressing would resemble a small blacking-brush, perhaps, but nothing entomological.

Then why, a persevering reader may ask, do I fish? Well, it is stronger than myself, the love of fishing; perhaps it is an inherited instinct, without the inherited power. I may have had a fishing ancestor who bequeathed to me the passion without the art. My vocation is fixed, and I have fished to little purpose all my days. Not for salmon, an almost fabulous and yet a stupid fish, which must be moved with a rod like a weaver's beam. The trout is more delicate and dainty – not the sea-trout, which any man, woman, or child can capture, but the yellow trout in clear water.

A few rises are almost all I ask for: to catch more than half a dozen fish does not fall to my lot twice a year. Of course, in a Sutherland loch one man is as good as another, the expert no better than the duffer. The fish will take, or they won't. If they won't, nobody can catch them; if they will, nobody can miss them. It is as simple as trolling a minnow from a boat in Loch Leven, probably the lowest possible form of angling.

41. A Lang 1895
A mysterious figure in Border hills

I plodded on with my labour, and went a-fishing when the day promised well. There was a hill loch (Loch Nan) about five miles away, which I favoured a good deal. The trout were large and fair of flesh, and in proper weather they rose pretty freely, and could be taken by an angler wading from the shore. There was no boat. The wading, however, was difficult and dangerous, owing to the boggy nature of the bottom, which quaked like a quicksand in some places. The black water, never stirred by duck or moorhen, the dry rustling reeds, the noisome smell of decaying vegetable-matter when you stirred it up in wading, the occasional presence of a dead sheep by the sullen margin of the tarn, were all opposed to cheerfulness. Still, the fish were *there*, and the 'lane,' which sulkily glided from the loch towards the distant river, contained some monsters, which took worm after a flood. One misty morning, as I had just topped the low ridge from which the loch became visible, I saw a man fishing from my favourite beach. Never had I noticed a human being there before, and I was not well pleased to think that some emissary of Mr Watson Lyall was making experiments in Loch Nan, and would describe it in 'The Sportsman's Guide.' The mist blew white and thick for a minute or two over the lochside, as it often does at Loch Skene; so white and thick and sudden that the bewildered angler there is apt to lose his way, and fall over the precipice of the *Grey Mare's Tail.* When the curtain of cloud rose again, the loch was lonely: the angler had disappeared. I went on rejoicing, and made a pretty good basket, as the weather improved and grew warmer – a change which gives an appetite to trout in some hill lochs. Among the sands between the stones on the farther bank I found traces of the angler's footsteps; he was not a phantom, at all events, for phantoms do not wear heavily nailed boots, as he evidently did. The traces, which were soon lost, of course, inclined 157 me to think that he had retreated up a narrow green burnside, with rather high banks, through which, in rainy weather, a small feeder fell into the loch. I guessed that he had been frightened away by the descent of the mist, which usually 'puts down' the trout and prevents them from feeding. In that case his alarm was premature. I marched homewards, happy with the unaccustomed weight of my basket, the contents of which were a welcome change from the usual porridge and potatoes, tea (without milk), jam, and scones of the shepherd's table. But, as I reached the height above the loch on my westward path, and looked back to see if rising fish were dimpling the still waters, all flushed as they were with sunset, behold, there was the Other Man at work again!

I should have thought no more about him had I not twice afterwards seen him at a distance, fishing up a 'lane' ahead of me, in the loneliest regions, and thereby, of course, spoiling my sport. I knew him by his peculiar stoop, which seemed not unfamiliar to me, and by his hat, which was of the clerical patten once known, perhaps still known, as 'a Bible-reader's' – a low, soft, slouched black felt. The second time that I found him thus anticipating me, I left off fishing and walked rather briskly towards him, to satisfy my curiosity, and ask the usual questions, 'What sport?' and 'What flies?' But as soon as he observed me coming he strode off across the heather. Uncourteous as it seems, I felt so inquisitive that I followed him. But he walked so rapidly, and was so manifestly anxious to shake me off, that I gave up the pursuit. Even if he were a poacher whose conscience smote him for using salmon-roe, I was not 'my brother's keeper,' nor anybody's keeper. He might 'otter' the loch, but how could I prevent him?

It was no affair of mine, and yet – where had I seen him before? His gait, his stoop, the carriage of his head, all seemed familiar – but a short-sighted man is accustomed to this kind of puzzle: he is always recognising the wrong person, when he does not fail to recognise the right one.

42. J MacVine 1891
An ungentlemanly angler

nglers, as a rule, are a genial and sociable class of men.
Occasionally one of a selfish and morose disposition is met
with, but such exceptions only prove the rule.

Such men generally possess little intelligence, and are void of
conversational powers. If they fish the same water as others their
object is to secure the first fishing of the most favourite pools, and to
enable them to do so are content with a *cold coffee* or milk breakfast
before sunrise. They hurry to the water, hurry over the pools in
succession, and thus frustrate their own selfish object, whilst those
who start some hours later, fishing slowly and carefully, will have the
advantage of them at the close of the day.

A man of the class referred to used at one time to fish on the Yair
waters. To enable him to be early on the river in a morning, he lodged at
a little cottage close by, and was generally in the water by sunrise.

It was a November morning, with a touch of frost and a thick mist
hanging along the course of the Tweed. The author reached the
'Moss Pool' shortly before eleven o'clock and caught two salmon of
sixteen pounds and eighteen pounds in it.

Towards two o'clock the *gentleman* referred to was returning from
the lower pools, when the question was put to him, 'Well, what
sport?' 'Nothing,' was his answer, 'what have *you* done?' On
receiving the information he said, 'That's queer! I fished the
"Moss Pool" early this morning and saw nothing.' 'Yes, I am quite
aware,' said the other, 'you wakened them out of their sleep, and
they were ready for breakfast when I arrived!'

Experience has proved that it is a mistake to run over a long stretch
of water. Two or three ordinary-sized pools, holding a fair stock of
fish, are sufficient for a day's fishing, providing the water is of a fair
size. By sticking to these, a fish or two will be got at some part of the
day, and much unnecessary exertion, by walking in heavy water-
proofs, as well as loss of time, will be avoided.

43. J MacVine 1891
A salmon under the ice

The scene which presented itself was such as might find a parallel only in the Arctic regions. The deep, smooth portions of the pools were covered with ice thick enough to carry an ox, and it was only in the rapid, streamy parts that there was any chance of wetting a line.

Between two long pools was a deep, rapid stream, comparatively free from ice in the centre. The opening might extend for twenty yards; and here the first line was cast, which immediately became coated with ice. As the fly approached the ice which covered the lower pool, the welcome tug was felt and joyously responded to. The fish, of sixteen pounds, ran merrily up the stream, evidently bent on reaching the upper pool. The tight line was just entering the ice, when it became evident that it must either get sawn through or broken. The angler at once put the point of his rod several feet deep in the water, and with a powerful strain held on till seventy yards of line were run out from the reel. At length symptoms of waning strength became manifest. The fish gradually yielded, till it was ultimately brought back and landed at the open water, where the ice at the edge had to be broken for that purpose.

When fishing at the same spot some few months later, a horse that was grazing in the field seemed to take some interest in the art of angling, and, coming quietly forward to the bank, quite unobserved by the angler, approached near enough to get caught by the fly.

Although pretty well accustomed to flies, it was evidently a stranger to such as had just fastened on its neck, and it started off, apparently very indignant at the unwarranted intrusion!

44. J MacVine 1891
Poachers' manners and morals.

T he poachers were watching them with evident delight. To one the author said, 'There's a grand run of fish going up to-day!' 'Ay,' said he exultingly, 'there's mair gaun up than will ever come doon!'

These poachers were fairly civil when spoken to in a pleasant matter, and it was of no use remonstrating with them – that was at once repudiated as being an undue interference with the rights of *labour*, and as they asserted that these fish were sent by Providence to feed hungry people in winter, when they could not work, they considered it no disgrace to be convicted and fined, or go to prison for a few weeks; indeed the lower and many of the middle classes looked on it as a venial offence, and a poacher when he came out of gaol was looked upon as a sort of martyr – a victim to the unjust laws of the country!

The lower classes might be actuated by *sinister* motives. They belonged to their class, and, better still, these poachers furnished them with an abundant supply of fresh salmon all the winter through at the low price of three-halfpence or twopence per pound.

Before the author became known in the district he was frequently accosted in the streets of Peebles: 'Will ye buy a nice *clean* salmon, sir? I'll sell ye ane cheap.' 'Is it *really* clean?' 'It's as bright and shining as a new shilling!' 'What do you want for it?' 'Sixpence the pund, sir!' 'No; I never buy salmon at this season.'

The rascals would have been delighted to take twopence per *pund*; but in many instances strangers were willing to buy them at sixpence, or more if it was asked.

The perseverance and ingenuity of these poachers were really worthy of a better cause; and had many of them displayed the same energy in a different calling they would no doubt have risen to eminence.

45. J MacVine 1891
Trolling for Salmon in Loch Tay

During the early months of the year Loch Tay has long been famed for the sport it affords in salmon fishing. It seems strange that this beautiful lake should stand almost alone in this respect. Some people account for it by asserting that it possesses a number of warm springs, which raise the temperature of the water, and this influence being felt by the fish as the water enters the sea, they follow it up till they reach comfortable quarters.

There is no doubt, whatever may be the cause, that an immense number of large salmon resort to it in January and February. The fishing, as a rule, continues fairly good up to the end of April, when it falls off to such an extent that few prosecute it at a later date.

The author has visited it twice in the month of February, with an interval of ten years intervening, and a good many more decades will expire before he could be induced to go there in February again.

Whatever may be the temperature of the water, that of the air is anything but inviting.

Ben Lawers and its brother 'Bens' are at that season usually coated with snow from base to summit. When to this is added a cutting east wind, it requires a strong effort of the imagination to make 'pleasure banish pain.'

Doubly coated, with a waterproof to boot, doubly flannelled and trebly hosed, doubly gloved, and muffled up to the ears, the fisher sits in a boat, 'from early morn till *frosty* eve,' watching the everlasting troll, troll, troll of his phantom minnows, ever and anon watching the points of his rods, and listening for the joyful sound of a big stone rattling down into the bottom of the boat. He feels himself to be the very embodiment of patience itself, not 'smiling at grief,' but most probably grinning at *shivers!* When the rattle of the big stone *does* startle the occupants of the boat, however, a bit of lively excitement succeeds, and a fight of an hour's duration is an event of common occurrence.

The first dash of the fish – if it should prove a lively one – may run out eighty or one hundred yards of line at a single rush; and if it takes a fancy to make a similar spin back towards the boat, the line of a necessity becomes slack, and the loose portion has to be wound up before it can be ascertained whether the fish is on or off. With three large tripod hooks attached to each minnow, however, they are generally pretty securely hooked, and a constant strain, combined with patience, ultimately brings it within reach, when it is gaffed into the boat.

The gaffing is an important part of the business, which is entrusted to the principal boatman, who may be called the 'gaffer' of the party; but it is an unpardonable offence to strike at the fish without bringing it into the boat.

With a blow or two from the mallet the fish gets its quietus, the hooks are extracted, and the man who has held the rod is congratulated on his good luck; the whisky is produced, and the boatmen quaff their bumper, with evident zest, to the toast, 'Here's health to men, and death to fish!'

'Returning home in triumph,' the capture is telegraphed to the 'Scotsman,' 'Glasgow Herald,' &c., and appears under the head of 'Angling' the following morning. Friends at a distance thus become aware of the important feat accomplished by Mr –, and he is complimented on being 'a great and successful salmon-fisher!'

46. J MacVine 1891
The author's superior skill and knowledge

H e took the rod and fished for a time, when he handed it back to its owner, who told him to go on and catch the fish that was lying beside the big stone. Mr Gillie tried hard, but said, 'That rod's ower soople to cast sae far; ye'd better tak it an' try it yersel.' Resuming the rod, and going a couple of yards backwards to obtain an easier angle, the author drew off eight or ten yards more line, and made the fly fall close to the opposite bank, when, with three steps and three casts more it came sweeping past the said stone, and was seized by a fifteen-pound salmon.

'Od, sir, ye have him!' said the gillie.

'Yes; shall I pull him straight out?'

'Na, na,' said he; 'ye maun *run* him!'

The gillie had brought his gaff, and went to the bankside with it ready for action, peering into the water with his keen little grey eyes, like a hawk about to pounce upon its prey, when he was asked, 'What are you going to do there?'

'I'll maybe get the cleek into him here if he comes near me.'

'No; you must not touch him; he must either be landed or lost without using the gaff.'

In due time the fish was exhausted, and floated into shallow water, when the angler lifted it out with his thread glove, saying, 'There, that's the way we do on Tweed!'

The gillies opened their eyes in amazement, and Number One said: 'Od, sir, that beats a'! 'Am thinking ye was just making fun o' us when ye pretended no ta ken how to cast yer line!'

All the best pools were fished, and the day passed without further sport. The gillie, having an eye to the prospective order for a dozen of his half-crown flies, was most attentive in pointing out all the best casts, which were carefully noted by the angler.

The following day Tweed flies only were used, when three fish were captured, weighing from eight pounds to sixteen pounds; so the order for flies was postponed *sine die!*

Tweed flies will kill on the Spey, and Spey flies will kill on the Tweed providing they are properly presented by any one who knows the lies of the fish.

The author has caught several salmon with a hook wrapped round with white cotton-wool for the body, no hackle, and some peacock harl tied down closely on the back. He has caught them with something like a 'Stewart worm-tackle,' having a bunch of teal feathers tied over them; and he is of opinion that *anything*, having the appearance of life, which approaches near enough to the lair of the fish when he is in a vindictive humour, will be seized.

47. W Scrope 1921
Salmon fishing disasters

Here ended my fishing, and in summing up the events of the day I had not much to congratulate myself upon. I had been guilty of almost every error possible. I broke my hook and my rod; I was moreover *cut* and *drowned*, technically speaking. I learned, however, four things: firstly, never to fish in a cast where the Kelpie has his stronghold; secondly, to look occasionally behind me before my throw, where the banks are steep and near; thirdly, to try the strength of my hook *before* I use it, not *after*; and, fourthly, to get into shoes of a proper consistency, and well studded with nails of Brobdingnag dimensions. Take warning, gentle readers, from these disasters, which are recounted for your benefit and instruction.

48. W Scrope 1921
Wading the river

Wading in the water is not only an agreeable thing in itself, but absolutely necessary in some rivers in the North that are destitute of boats; and that you may do this in the best possible style, procure half a dozen pair of shoes, with large knob-nails at some distance asunder: if they are too close, they will bring your foot to an even surface, and it will glide off a stone or rock, which in deep water may be inconvenient. Cut some holes in the upper-leathers of your shoes, to give the water a free passage out of them when you are on dry land; not because the fluid is annoying, for we should wrong you to say so, but to prevent the pumping noise you would otherwise make at every step. If you are not much of a triton, you may use fishermen's boots, and keep yourself dry: it is all a matter of taste. When you are wading through the rapids, step on quickly and boldly, and do not gaze down on the stream after the fashion of Narcissus; for running waves will not reflect your beauty, but only make your head giddy. If you stop for a moment, place your legs abreast of each other: should you fancy a straddle, with one of them in advance, the action of the water will operate upon both, trip you up, and carry you out to sea. Observe, I am talking of a heavy stream.

49. W Scrope 1921
Casting and fishing the salmon fly

C asting the fly is a knack, and cannot well be taught but by experience: the spring of the rod should do the chief work, and not the labour of your arm. To effect this, you should lay the stress as near the hand as possible, and make the wood undulate from that point; which is done by keeping your elbow in advance, and doing something with your wrist, which, as Mr Penn says, is not very easy to explain. Thus the exertion should be chiefly from the elbow and wrist, and not from the shoulders. You should throw clear beyond the spot where the salmon lie, so that they may not see the fly light upon the water; then you should bring the said fly round the stream, describing the segment of a circle taking one step in advance at every throw. In this manner the fish see your fly only, and not the line. It is customary to give short jerks with the fly as you bring it round, something in the manner of minnow fishing, but in a more gentle and easy way; and I think this manner is the most seducing you can adopt: it sets the wings in a state of alternate expansion and contraction that is extremely captivating.

50. W Scrope 1921
Salmon fishing needs strength rather than patience

As for myself, if I am ever so indiscreet as to utter a word about fishing, I am always asked, 'if it does not require a great deal of patience.'

I say then, and will maintain it, that a salmon fisher should be strong in the arms, or he will never be able to keep on thrashing for ten or twelve hours together with a rod eighteen or twenty feet long, with ever and anon a lusty salmon at the end of his line, pulling like a wild horse with the lasso about him. Now he is obliged to keep his arms aloft, that the line may clear the rocks – now he must rush into the river, then back out with nimble pastern, always keeping a steady and proper strain of line; and he must preserve his self-possession, 'even in the very tempest and whirlwind of the sport,' when the salmon rushes like a rocket. This is not moody work; it keeps a man alive and stirring. Patience indeed!

51. W Scrope 1921
Playing a large salmon

When you get hold of a *monstrum horrendum ingens* of a fish, say of some five and forty pounds, you must anticipate a very long and severe battle. If, therefore, you have a disposable Gilly with you, despatch him instantly for some skilful fisherman, as well to assist you when you are exhausted with fatigue, as to bring your dinner and supper; not forgetting a dark lantern, that you may not be beaten by the shades of night – a circumstance by no means improbable. At the first onset you will probably be obliged to keep your arms and rod aloft, in order to steer clear of the rocks. This action, with a heavy rod and large fish on your line, is very distressing, if continued even for a short time; and it will be necessary to repeat it often, if the channel is not very favourable; and in that case your muscles will ache insupportably, if they at all resemble those of other men. The easiest position, when it is safe to use it, is to place the butt of your rod against the stomach as a rest, and to bring the upper part of the arm and the elbow in close contact with the sides, putting on at the same time an air of determination.

If your leviathan should be superlatively boisterous, no one knows what may happen.

52. W Scrope 1921
A Tweed baillie wi' a conscience

I f I were to write an account of half the poaching tricks that are common to all Salmon rivers, I should produce a book, the dimensions of which would terrify the public, even in this pen-compelling age.

In times when water bailiffs in Tweed had very small salaries, they themselves were by no means scrupulous about the observance of close time, but partook of the good things of the river in all seasons, lawful or unlawful. There is a man now, I believe, living at Selkirk, who in times of yore used certain little freedoms with the Tweed Act, which did not become the virtue of his office. As a water bailiff he was sworn to tell of all he saw; and indeed, as he said, it could not be expected that he should tell of what he did not see.

When his dinner was served up during close time, his wife usually brought to the table in the first place a platter of potatoes and a napkin; she then bound the latter over his eyes that nothing might offend his sight. This being done, the illegal salmon was brought in smoking hot, and he fell to, blindfolded as he was, like a conscientious water bailiff – if you know what that is; nor was the napkin taken from his eyes till the fins and bones were removed from the room, and every visible evidence of a salmon having been there had completely vanished: thus he saw no illegal act committed, and went to give in his annual report at Cornhill with his idea of a clear conscience. This was going too near the wind, or rather the water; but what would you have? – the man was literal, and a great eater of Salmon from his youth.

53. W Scrope 1921
Si non, quocunque modo

Ill this to the Southern ear sounds like poaching of the most flagitious description; but a salmon is a fish of passage, and if you do not get him to-day he will be gone to-morrow. The Tweed used to let for above £12,000 a year; judge, then, in what a wholesale manner these fish are caught by long nets and other sweeping modes; yet in what profusion they continue to be found! You may just as well think of preserving herrings or mackerel as these delicious creatures; and there would be no objection to your taking 3378 salmon at one haul, if fortune would so favour you, as Commander Ross did at Boothia Felix on the 26th of July, 1831.

Keep *Close time* strictly; kill no spawning fish; tamper not with foul ones of any sort; preserve the fry; send the black fishers to Iceland; but catch as many salmon as you can, *recte si possis* (meaning with a rod), *si non, quocunque modo* – that is, with a net or leister, and so forth.

54. W C Stewart 1958
Angling is healthy

A ngling, when once embarked in by any person possessed of a reasonable amount of soul and brains, becomes a passion, and like other passions will grow and feed upon the smallest possible amount of encouragement. Fish or no fish, whenever opportunity offers, the angler may be found at the water-side. If this only went on in fine weather, people could understand it, but nowadays, even in summer, the weather is not always fine; and when a man is seen standing in the water for hours in a torrent of rain, with benumbed hands and an empty basket, doubts of the individual's sanity naturally suggest themselves, mixed with feelings of pity for the terrible consequences in the way of colds, rheumatism, &c., which it is supposed must inevitably follow, but which don't. We have it from high medical authority, that rheumatism is more engendered by hot rooms and fires than by exposure, and as for the comfort of the thing, that is according to taste. It is surely better to have fresh air and exercise, even in wet, than to be spending the whole day in some country inn, yawning over some second-rate novel for the third time.

55. W C Stewart 1958
Fishing to catch fish

S ome anglers have also a habit of characterising large takes as butchery; the point where sport stops and butchery commences lying about the individual's greatest take. We cannot see the justice of an opinion that considers the capture of a certain number of trout sport, and of twice that number – taken by the same means – butchery. If the sport of angling lies in the capture of fish, it seems evident that the more fish the better sport; and it is our intention to treat of the different branches of angling solely with the view of showing how the greatest weight of trout can be captured in a given time. There are not many days from May till October, in which an angler, thoroughly versed in all the mysteries of the craft, should not kill at least twelve pounds weight of trout in any county in the south of Scotland, not excepting Edinburghshire itself. And to describe the way in which this may be done is our object in this small volume.

56. W C Stewart 1958
A stiff rod is essential

The two great requisites in a rod we consider to be stiffness and lightness, two qualities exceedingly difficult to combine. The amount of stiffness should be such that, when casting, the forward motion of the rod may be stopped pretty quickly without any recoil of the point taking place. Most of the rods that are to be had ready made in Edinburgh are useless from their excessive pliability, and from what we have seen of English and Irish rods they are still worse. This is not the fault of the rod-makers, who require to suit the public taste, but the fault of anglers who will have their rods made in that manner. We know of no place where a better rod can be had than in Edinburgh if the angler only says that he wishes it stiff. In casting with a supple rod, after propelling the line forward, and stopping the forward motion of the hand, a recoil of the point takes place, which to a considerable extent interferes with the forward motion of the line.

The advantages of a stiff rod are its great superiority in casting; it will throw a longer and a lighter line, and with greater certainty, to any spot the angler wishes. Its advantages, in these respects, are particularly apparent in a windy day, when it is necessary to cast against the wind, or even sideways to it. With a supple rod, in such circumstances, it is almost impossible to get the line out at all.

57. W C Stewart 1958
The skill of James Baillie

J ames Baillie, whom we have already introduced to the reader, but whose hazel rod and string tied to the top of it were familiar to all those in the habit of frequenting Leader or Gala, maintained himself and family from March to November by fly-fishing exclusively. We believe this notable person killed on an average from twelve to fourteen pounds at each excursion, and, being in delicate health, he only fished for four or five hours a day. If our amateur friends had to make their living by fly-fishing, there are few of them we would care for dining with often.

Besides being the most attractive and valuable, artificial fly-fishing is the most difficult branch of the angler's art, and this is another reason of the preference accorded to it, since there is more merit, and therefore more pleasure, in excelling in what is difficult.

58. W C Stewart 1958
To fish upstream is essential

We believe we are not beyond the mark in stating that ninety-nine anglers out of a hundred fish down with the artificial fly; they never think of fishing in any other way, and never dream of attributing their want of success to it. Yet we are prepared to prove, both in theory and practice, that this is the greatest reason of their want of success in clear waters. In all our angling excursions we have only met one or two amateurs and a few professionals, who fished up stream with the fly, and used it in a really artistic manner. If the wind is blowing up, anglers will occasionally fish up the pools – (as for fishing up a strong stream they never think of it) – but even then they do not do it properly, and meet with little better success than if they had followed their usual method. They will also, if going to some place up a river, walk up, not fish up to it – their plan being to go to the top of a pool, and then fish it down, never casting their line above them at all.

We shall now mention in detail the advantages of fishing up, in order to show its superiority over the old method.

59. W C Stewart 1958
The errors of 'downstreamers'

O thers object to fishing up stream, as requiring too frequent casting, being too fatiguing, and because they have been accustomed to fish down, and would prefer fishing in that way, even though they do not catch so many trout. If any angler prefers catching five pounds weight of trout fishing down stream, to ten pounds weight fishing up, we may wonder at his taste, but it is no concern of ours. Our duty is to point out how most trout can be captured in a given time; and that is by fishing up stream, and such is now the method adopted by all the best fly-fishers of the day.

Those anglers who have adopted fishing up stream are principally those who were adepts in the old system, and who were possessed of all the nicety in casting and other knowledge so essential to successful up-stream fishing.

60. W C Stewart 1958
Scottish trouting superior to English

I n comparing the severity of the fishing in Scotch and English streams, it must be borne in mind that the former are, as a rule, open to the public, and that the latter, as a rule, are preserved, and fished only by a favoured few. If Mr Francis will point out any stream in England, in which he thinks it worth while to throw a fly for trout, that is more and better fished than Tweed and its tributaries, we shall be very much surprised. And on behalf of Scotch anglers we repudiate with scorn the bare idea that it requires less skill to catch a Scotch trout than an English one, or that the former in any way receives an inferior education as regards flies, etc., to his English brother. In fact, we believe that in the before-mentioned streams the education of the inhabitants is as superior to that of the inhabitants of English streams as the education of the people of the one country is admitted to be to that of the other; and supposing the most accomplished believer in the English theory – ay, even Mr Francis himself – engaged on a mile of Tweed along with twenty or thirty Galashiels weavers (by no means an unusual number), we question if his basket at the finish would illustrate very strongly the superiority of his theory and practice. We have met English anglers even in Scotland counting their takes by the brace, and not in much danger of going wrong in their reckoning either.

61. W C Stewart 1958
Concentrate on the matter in hand

I f you are tired, or the trout are not taking, sit down and console yourself in some way or other. A late writer upon the subject suggests that for this purpose the angler should carry a New Testament in his pocket, to which there can be no possible objection, but we rather think most anglers prefer spiritual consolation of a very different sort, coupled with sandwiches; there is a time for all things, and at noon we must admit having a preference for the latter method. It has, moreover, this advantage, that you will be the more able to fish properly when the trout begin to take again.

62. W C Stewart 1958
Worming is a summer sport

A s July draws to a close, trout do not take the worm so well –
they begin to be capricious, and will sometimes take only for
an hour or two in the forenoon; so that worm-fishing in our
earlier streams may be said to be at an end; and if the angler continues
it through August, he must have recourse to the more backward
districts, and sometimes even to hill-burns. We have known excellent
worm-fishers unable to capture a dozen trout in the end of August,
where a month earlier they could with ease have filled a basket. And
worm fishing may be limited to six weeks or two months in summer –
the time varying according to the season, for which the best guide we
can give the angler is, that it generally commences about a week after
the Mayflies are done, and in streams where these flies do not exist
about the beginning of June.

63. W C Stewart 1958
A fancy minnow tackle

O n such occasions we have found a drag, consisting of two No. 10 hooks tied back to back, and left to play loose about three inches behind the minnow, very effective. Some anglers put a drag-hook about half an inch behind the tail, in expectation of those trout that bite short taking hold of this hook with their mouth, but this rarely happens. The tail of the minnow in spinning describes a considerable circumference, and the drag, being farther out, a still greater one; so that, if the trout misses the minnow, there is little chance of its catching the drag. The drag which we advise should be dressed on a separate piece of gut, sufficiently long to keep it a least three inches behind the minnow, and attached to the upper hook of the minnow-tackle by a loop, so that it may be taken off or put on at pleasure. The object of having it so far behind the minnow is to catch, by the outside of the body, those trout which bite shy or miss the minnow.

64. W C Stewart 1958
Loch-fishing is easy and not so tiring

A ll these things render loch-fishing a less difficult, and consequently less interesting, branch of angling than fishing in our southern streams. It is, indeed, the simplest fishing of any, and the one in which the tyro and the accomplished angler are most upon a par; and we do not wonder that most good anglers prefer capturing smaller but more wary trout in southern streams, to larger and better trout in some remote loch. Still loch-fishing has its advantages. It is not nearly so fatiguing as river-fishing, and therefore better adapted for some.

65. W C Stewart 1958
Troll if you must

T rolling is dull work, as it is by no means uncommon for an angler to toil a whole day without getting a single specimen, and even when successful the merit of the capture lies partly with the boatman, who knows the places and rows the boat. Unless the loch is too stormy to fish with fly, we would never advise anyone to devote himself to trolling exclusively, but when on the loch it is as well to be provided with a trolling rod and tackle, and to use it when rowing from one place to another, thus filling up the intervals during which he cannot use the fly.

66. T T Stoddart 1847
Waders, especially for the older angler

W ading Boots. – It is quite true, that, in my younger days, I regarded these a cumbersome and unnecessary part of my equipment, and so they would prove in all pedestrian excursions, undertaken by juvenile anglers, in the hey-day of health and vigour; but as one becomes sobered down, and more chary of his exertions, he not only reconciles himself to their use, but actually feels out of place in their absence. To a salmon fisher who has no boat at command, and who, to obtain sport, requires to plunge knee-deep in the element, during the months of March and April, as well as October, in seasons, in fact, when the temperature is by no means high, they are absolutely necessary; and even to the trout fisher, in May and June, who is liable to suffer from habitual exposure to wet, they constitute a desirable means of protection.

Trout flies simplified

L och flies for trout, I have as yet only alluded to, nor is a great deal required to be said upon this subject. In common with river flies, they are capable of being reduced to two or three varieties. These, in their simple state, are, as before-mentioned, the black hackle, the red or brown ditto, and hare-lug fly. A division however, so very primitive and elemental, when applied to loch flies is apt, I am aware, to be ridiculed and sneered at by pedants in the art; nor in fact, do I intend it, in practice, to be pushed to the extreme. It is only tasteful and becoming to admit variety into the fly assortment, provided this variety be placed under proper control. When I allude therefore to the hackles in question, as forming along with the hare-lug the only flies required by the angler, I wish it to be understood that the fundamental, I do not say requisite, portion of the dressing consists of the material after which the hook is named. It cannot be denied that, in the case of the hackle fly, the wing, tinsel, and dubbing, whether of silk or wool, possess, on many occasions, an attractive influence over trout, nay, even a combination of these without hackle at all, may constitute a taking lure; but what is proved by all this but that fish are allured, not on account of the close resemblance which the artificial hook is designed to have to particular insects appropriate to particular months and seasons, but from other causes of a different nature? These are size, motion, form and colour; the latter qualification being the one upon which, by introducing certain well-tried standards, my classification, as regards the artificial fly, has been conducted.

68. T T Stoddart 1847
Fishing the worm upstream

A s I have already had occasion to remark, all able worm-fishers invariably cast the line up the stream, taking their stance below where the trout are presumed to lie, and never allowing the bait, as it is carried down by the current, to pass beneath them. This practice of theirs embodies two separate advices, both of which respectively demand attention. In heaving the bait up against the course of the stream, more than one advantage accrues to the angler. He is, first of all, kept better concealed from the wary eye of the trout, which, as is well known, always, when resting, fronts the current; and although possessed of visual organs sufficiently prominent to detect objects above or on either side of it, can descry but very partially what takes place in its rear. Again, from his position, he can strike with greater effect. In this particular he acquires a very decided advantage over the old-fangled mode of worm-fishing, that, namely, of casting down the stream; adopting which system the angler, when striking, is more apt to pull his hook fairly out of the mouth of the fish without even pricking it than, as when he throws against the current and strikes downward, to bring it, bend and barb, into direct contact with the open jaws of the bitter. A third advantage obtained by the mode of casting I am recommending is, that the water is less disturbed; the unavoidable plunging of the wader affecting only those portions of it that lie below him, and which he has either thought proper to omit as useless, or has already ransacked.

69. T T Stoddart 1847
Salmon roe for trout is sometimes justifiable

Although fishing with the salmon roe is considered, and perhaps with reason, by many anglers, as allied to poaching, and in consequence is frequently tiraded against, without pause or forbearance, I do not think I should be doing justice to what is designed to be a full exposition of the art and science of angling were I to exclude all notice of it from these pages. The wonderful property possessed by the bait in question, of attracting trout is, of itself, a subject demanding the attention and investigation of the naturalist. To what sense or instinct inherent in the fish it is attributable remains still, in some measure, a matter of dispute; whether, in fact, it is dependent upon the exquisiteness of their taste, or that subtle power of discernment which not unfrequently is connected with the organ of smell. For my own part, I am inclined to believe it depends upon the exercise of both senses, although chiefly upon the latter. That the use of the salmon roe in its prepared state as employed by anglers, possesses the virtue I speak of to a truly singular extent, a very few instances falling under personal experience may suffice to prove, and from these, I undertake to make a few deductions in favour of, occasionally and in certain localities, employing it as a bait for trout.

Its wholesale use, however, without respect to river and season, I utterly condemn, in common with all lovers of fair sport; and although, on the occasions to be made mention of, some may deem that I advance far towards transgressing upon the principle I profess to hold, they will find, if I mistake not, in my argument, a good and sufficient apology.

70. T T Stoddart 1847
A gigantic eel from Tweed

T here was evidently something attached to it of considerable weight and bulk, without, however, any live resistance. Imagine my surprise, when, on hauling it nearer the bank, I beheld a huge eel enveloped among the cords, quite choked and lifeless. Of river eels it was the largest I had ever witnessed, although I certainly have seen congers of greater size. Above four feet and a half in length, and in girth fully eleven inches, I think it could not have weighed less than twenty pounds. This point, however, I wanted the ready means of determining, although I regret not having made an effort to acquaint myself with it. On examining the stomach of the monster, I found that it contained all the three gorge-hooks employed by me, and the trouts with which, individually, they had been baited. My experience in eel fishing has not been very great, but I have taken some hundreds of them in my time, and I do not remember above one or two that showed fight in the same manner this one did, while on the rod.

71. T T Stoddart 1847
'Snatching' Salmon in the Dochart at Killin.

S almon also ascend it, but not in large numbers, as they are greatly obstructed by a water-fall of considerable height, near the mouth of the river, at Killin. This fall is an object of equal interest to the fisher and the scene-hunter. The former may here practise, if inclined, a mode of angling for salmon, which, although it does not test the caprice of the fish, or even the skill of the fisherman, yet affords, under the circumstances of the case, legitimate sport. The apparatus used is simply a strong rod or staff, to which are appended a cord and heavy plummet, along with a set of large hooks, 'tria juncta in uno.' These, the angler taking his position on a rock close to the cataract, drop into the foaming water below, the spot where the salmon generally rest having been pointed out to him. On the plummet coming into contact with the bottom he merely requires to give a jerk upwards with his rod and should a fish, which frequently happens, be in the way, he has every chance of getting hold of it. I have seen the same mode of fishing practised in the Orrin in Ross-shire, and I understand that, in certain states of water, it proves very successful.

72. T T Stoddart 1866
Miscellany of snippets from the Rambles

'A miserably clad wild-looking object, the expression of whose features was that of confirmed idiocy blended to some extent with cunning. . . Ugh! Ugh! or Gaelic monosyllable . . . accompanied by violent gestures, not one of them a whit more intelligible . . .' (p. 60, Sassenach view of a typical Highlander)

'. . . to my fondness for, scenery taken by itself, I fear I am too far implicated in the piscatorial mania to do proper justice . . .' (p. 62, the normal view)

'. . . my frail ear was subjected, for at least the space of four mortal hours, to a course of laments and pibrochs . . . such a musical agony I have never since endured . . . that union of howling uproar, with frantic gesticulation, which forms the soul and spirit of the highland dance . . .' (pp. 86–87, more Sassenach prejudice)

'. . . that persecuted bird whose proper treatment gives almost arable value to the dreariest moorland . . .' (p. 85, not a shooting man)

'. . . is too nice in his distinctions and too fond of amplification . . . the endeavour made by him . . . in that curious production entitled *Fish and Fishing in the Lone Glens of Scotland* . . . to derange, as far as it has been established, the natural history of the Salmonidae . . .' (pp. 110–111, a good anti-Knox gibe).

'. . . with the hatred and calumny of a displaced tenantry . . . and with the prejudices, low cunning and indolent habits of that class . . .' (p. 143, yet more Sassenach prejudice)

'. . . laziness . . . religious arrogance . . . gloomy, sanctimonious cast of countenance and a stern, overbearing manner . . . smattering of Scriptural erudition . . .' (p. 146, of Highland lairdies)

'. . . Stewart's patterns . . . are simply revivals of the old Lothian persuaders and have no more claim to originality of design than his method of worm fishing . . . in vogue forty years ago and upwards . . .' (p. 172, elsewhere he called Stewart 'the Pretender')

'. . . I feel quite convinced that the substitution of salmon gut . . . for the clumsy traces usually employed and by use of brass swivels and revolving baits, a step will be taken towards rendering sea fishing an exciting and delightful amusement . . .' (p. 343, well ahead of his time)

AN ANGLER'S RAMBLES

AND

ANGLING SONGS

BY THOMAS TOD STODDART

AUTHOR OF 'THE ANGLER'S COMPANION TO THE RIVERS AND LOCHS OF SCOTLAND.'

EDINBURGH
EDMONSTON & DOUGLAS
MDCCCLXVI.

73. T T Stoddart 1866
In difficulties on the Spey

A fter lashing for three successive days, without the ghost of a rise, the stretch of water assigned to me, which I admit, however, was in galloping humour, and quite out of order the whole time, I began to conclude that I had come to Fochabers on a fool's errand. As a final resort I took to trout-fishing, with results which did not exceed my expectation, and were quite on a par with the very unpromising nature of the channel, which, until on its approach to Garmouth, where the river becomes split up into several currents, is of the barest description, void of nutriment and shelter-places. The generality of the trout, in consequence, are not much longer than one's finger. Lower down, where the Spey is broken up into sections, and islands have been formed, covered over with brushwood, the shelter and feeding-grounds improve; but the class of trout peopling the runs and side-stretches which there abound is not in keeping with the appearance of the place; nor did I find it an easy task to force my way through the tangled bushes, and over the uneven ground, strewn with drift-wood, which form part and pertinent of the north bank of the river.

74. T T Stoddart 1866
Stoddart's hatred of the pipes

A t dinner, the ceremony of saying grace was finished off, if not wholly conducted, by the chieftain's own piper, who strutted up and down the narrow space assigned to him with an air of dignity assimilated to that of the moor-cock itself, when in full courting plumage. A cover removed, and grouse soup, with other preliminaries, discussed, in marched the kilted retainer a second time, venting from his inflated instrument a succession of groans and skirls, of ear-torturing and brain-confusing sounds, which, had my attention not been drawn to the effect they had upon the chieftain himself, would have led me to judge of Highland music as an outrage upon taste and common sense. There is something, certainly, which it is not easy to account for, in the accommodation given by the ear, when brought into contact with them, to the tones of the bagpipe. I can understand how in the distance they exercise a fascinating influence over the Highlander, and where the connexion holds good betwixt Gaelic music and the voices which pervade the glens and mountains – the wail of the blast, the rush and roar of the waterfall, the thunder echo, the plaintive cry of the curlew, the scream of the eagle, the bellowing of the stag, and the many sounds familiar to the ear in the land of flood and heath. I can appreciate its power in the battle-field as an animating medium, and can recognise something even of a martial spirit in its shrill and discordant strains; but how, when pent up within the walls of a small apartment, it should not only become tolerated, but made use of as a source of stirring pleasure, is past comprehension.

75. T T Stoddart 1866
Lost near Loch Lyon

On July 22nd I passed over a heathy tract of country to the Lyon Water, which communicates with the Tay. The morning on which I set out was tolerably clear, but I well recollect how, on gaining the heights above Loch Rannoch, a mist settled down round about; then succeeded a kind of drizzle, which gradually lapsed into rain and violent wind. There was at that time no road, and the landmarks I was counselled to steer by were entirely shrouded up. In a wild, lonesome country, abounding in swamps – and there are scarcely any in Scotland drearier in their character, and more to be dreaded than those in the neighbourhood of the moor of Rannoch – the feeling of losing one's way is by no means agreeable. I was in this predicament to a certain extent, but I had a long stretch of daylight before me, as well as the advantage which was given by the wind's blowing steadily in one direction. Thus favoured, I pressed on with a resolution which only began to waver after a ten hours' march, when the sensation of tiredness took possession of my limbs, and that bewildering feeling crept over me which few who have not been similarly circumstanced can have a correct notion of. At this juncture, and just as I was on the point of stretching my soaked and exhausted limbs on the heather, a break in the cloud overhead betokened the bursting forth of the afternoon's sun. The change, I need not say, acted like a spell. I was at the river's edge, in the heart of Glen Lyon, almost at a bound; and in the course of a few minutes my rod and line were busy at work over the swollen stream.

76. T T Stoddart 1866
On the river Dochart

From Loch Tay I passed on to Killin, amusing myself for an hour in the Lochy, a short way above where it enters the Dochart. Rains having fallen on the high grounds during the night, this stream, which above the point of junction is of a level character, was in good order, and invitingly ruffled. The trout in consequence rose freely. At Killin I spent some time watching the mode of catching salmon practised at the Bridge Pool. I then struck up the valley of the Dochart towards Luib, wetting feather occasionally on the river as I proceeded. The day had become too bright and calm to expect sport with the fly, no discoloration from rain, such as had affected its feeder, having taken place in the main stream. As a trouting river, the Dochart was held in high estimation by the late Professor Wilson, and formed, in the neighbourhood of Luib, the scene of one of his last angling explorations, in 1845. The rod-fishing for salmon, I may mention, on the Dochart, near Luib, during summer, is more to be relied on than what at that season is met with in Strath-Tay itself. To account for this, besides the presence of the fish, and such facilities as are given by the reduced size and natural boarding up of the river, in the way of commanding the salmon-casts, there is to be taken into consideration the lower temperature of the water, incident to the altitude of its course, during the hot months.

77. T T Stoddart 1866
Fly tying extemporised

O ur provision for the morrow's sport . . . had been reduced to one or two doubtful patterns; the favourite one, a green-bodied dun-wing, having been so sorely mauled in the evening's tussle as to prove unfit for further service.

A visit to the inn poultry-yard helped to put us in possession, fortunately, of feathers, hackles included, which, although of a coarse description, approximated in point of colour to what was desired; and with a twitch or two of green worsted abstracted from the parlour crumbcloth, we contrived to make up half a dozen as deadly persuaders as ever issued from the fingers of an Evatt or a Blacker; at least so, next day, notwithstanding their somewhat unartistic appearance, they proved to be. We were favoured, on the occasion of using them, with a fine breeze; the river also was in good trim; – circumstances which assisted, no doubt, to put us in conceit of our workmanship.

The result on the 10th was in keeping with the highest expectations of sport we had been led to form in regard to this river as the resort of sea-trout. My friend Wilson, however, met with by far the larger share of success – a result owing partly to this superior skill, and partly to the fact of his strictly confining himself to that particular range of water which, in all salmon rivers, may be set down as the *habitat* of the sea-trout when in good condition.

78. T T Stoddart 1866
Loch Laggan with Wilson

While quartering here, my friend Wilson was directed by our host to a small lake and its connecting rivulet, on the opposite side of Loch Laggan, to reach which, there being no boat at command, he had to wade the shoal at the mouth of the Pattaig. From this mountain tarn it was dark long before he returned; and as he had to repass the ford alluded to, no little anxiety was expressed on his account. He came safely back, however, with not only his creel, but his handkerchief and pockets crammed with trout, twenty-six dozens in all, which, averaging them at one-fourth of a pound each, and the average I think was heavier, speaks to seventy-eight pounds. On the day of this extraordinary take, the result both of judgment and great perseverance, I clung to the banks of the Pattaig, and such portions of Loch Laggan in the vicinity of the inn as could be fished with some chance of success from the margins. In the Pattaig I was disappointed, as I had been led, from its position as main feeder to the lake, and from its being in fairish trim, to expect sport in the way of large trout, which, I thought it probable, would at that season of the year have crowded into it in search of food, if not for the purpose of pairing. After beating, however, this river for two hours, during which, although I encreeled two or three dozens of lean, shabby trout, no monster showed face, I abandoned it, without gaining much by the change.

79. T T Stoddart 1866
Boyhood trouting near Edinburgh, ca 1825

The Water of Leith, however, was my favourite resort on these occasions. With the exception of a few pools above Slateford, the whole of this stream was, at the time I speak of, open to the angling fraternity. I was in the habit of thrashing it unchallenged all the way up from St Bernard's Well to Little Vantage. Although the prime portions of this stream lay above Malleny, on which range I have taken, in the course of a day's fishing, as many as five or six dozens of yellow trout, yet on the very skirts of Edinburgh sport was occasionally met with. At Coltbridge, trout were then not only numerous, but of a respectable size. I recollect seeing one exhibited at a shop in Rose Street which weighed eight pounds. This fish was taken with a midge-fly at the mouth of a water-course, used for the purposes of irrigation, which entered the river on the South side, within a few yards of the Corstorphine road.

80. T T Stoddart 1866
Wind-lines on Loch Luichart

D uring a residence of some months in the neighbourhood of Contin, I frequently laid this lake under contribution. It took my fancy, as much on account of the scenery by which it is approached, and its own pastoral beauty, as of the sport it afforded. Under a good smart breeze, which chafed the margins, and caused the formation of foam-lines on the surface, an effect which every angler must have witnessed again and again, the trout usually rose well. These lines or streaks, when the wind happens to be travelling steadily up or down the loch (the form of many of our Highland reservoirs admits, in regard to its direction, the use of such terms), hold a parallel relation to the water's edge, and lie at a distance from it, regulated by the marginal indentations, force of air, etc., – sometimes at an arm's length, sometimes as far from the shore as one can manage to cast. Occasionally, in very gusty weather, when the surface of the water is hit in a particular way, the whole bosom of the lake becomes ribbed over with them; but in this case they are of no telling advantage, whereas, when they are strictly marginal, they exercise an attractive power over the fish, disposing them to look out for surface-food, and approach the water's edge for this purpose.

81. T T Stoddart 1866
Flies tied for the Professor by James Wright

A s the medium, to a limited extent, of getting it up, I was honoured a few years before his death with a request to select, or rather give an order for, and superintend the dressing of a gross of artificial trouting-flies, which should comprehend most of the specimens approved of on Tweedside. As an expert and ready hand, I employed James Wright of Sprouston, describing to him by the assistance of his specimen-book what was likely to give satisfaction. In point of variety, my selection was limited to a dozen sorts or thereabouts, two or three sizes of each, ranging on the Adlington scale from No. 0 up to No. 7 or 8. There were comprised in it the spring-flies, white-tips, and the three varieties of March-brown; black, red, dun, partridge and grouse hackles; peacock-tail, fur and silk bodies, with their appendages in the shape of wing, taken from the woodcock, starling, mallard, landrail, lark, etc., etc. This selection, with which the late Professor expressed himself highly pleased, was, I have reason to believe, shortly afterwards drawn upon and put to the test on the Dochart near Luib, and Loch Awe, not far from Port Sonachan. The results are recorded in his own words in the Memoir of his Life by Mrs Gordon. It was the last occasion on which the sporting jacket of this great and gifted man, an athlete in body as well as mind, was donned, or his magical wand waved over terrestrial river.

82. T T Stoddart 1866
Tibby and her hospitable house

But Tibby Shiels – who is Tibby Shiels? and what connexion has Tibby with St Mary's Loch? Considering her sphere of life and action, Tibby is perhaps, be it chronicled, one of the most noted and notable women alive. For forty years she has been the occupant of a cottage which consisted, when I first knew it, of little more than a *butt* and a *ben*, along with garret accommodation; but, circumstances requiring and means permitting, it has, since then, undergone many alterations, and affords, in its present state, comfortable night-quarters to a large party of anglers. This rural retreat is situated on a piece of meadow land which divides St Mary's Loch from a small sheet of water, aptly called, from its position, the Loch of the Lowes or Lochs. It is not a hostelry – never was. Its frequenters are presumed to provide, in the matter of exciseable fluids, their own cheer, and this in one respect is of advantage, as it retains in the hands of the landlady a discretionary power of admitting or refusing lodgers, whereas, where the premises are licensed, that privilege becomes questionable, or at least greatly hampered in its exercise. The cottage of Tibby Shiels, *alias* Mrs Richardson (it is the custom among the heights of the Border land for widows in the humbler condition of life to resume or consent to the resumption of their maiden names, and the worthy old lady, although the mother of a pretty numerous family, of course succumbs to it), along with the surrounding park or cow-grass, belongs to that most amiable of men, and able of diplomatists, Lord Napier.

83. T T Stoddart 1866
Conviviality at Tibby's place

I t formed . . . one of the pretences for a protracted *gaudeamus,*
the term applied to those jovial merry-makings with which, on
a meeting of congenial souls, the day was usually wound up. It
must not be supposed, however, that under Tibby's roof these
symposia, although frequently indulged in, degenerated at any time
into scenes of drunken riot. Although whisky-toddy was in circula-
tion, as the beverage best suited to that upland region, and refresh-
ingly exhilarating above all others to the angler, after a hearty meal
on his return from the water's side, it was always, as far as I can
recollect, imbibed with propriety and in moderation; its invariable
effects being to promote good fellowship, and from reserved natures
to elicit sparks, from open ones to draw flashes of intelligence and
joyous humour, which had else, without its inspiring influence, never
come to light. The occasional presence of the Ettrick Shepherd at
these meetings assisted rather to relieve them than otherwise, of a
bacchanalian tendency; and although we were inclined, when so
favoured, in spite of the gentle remonstrances of our worthy landlady, to prolong them to a late hour, it was seldom at the risk of being
constrained to encounter more than an *extra* tumbler, in return for
which outrage self-inflicted upon our temperate habits, we were sure
to be gratified, on demand, with a lilt from the poet. His favourites,
which I have heard him give voice to above a score of times, and he
did so invariably with a heartiness of expression that counterbalanced
any little defect there might be of musical taste or ear, were his well-
known rendering of the Jacobite air, 'Prince Charlie,' or 'Cam ye by
Athol,' and that simple but beautiful love-lay, headed, 'When the kye
comes hame.'

84. T T Stoddart 1866
Stoddart's biggest Fish and others on Tweed

One of the most severe runs I ever recollect meeting with took place below the Thorn-tree Nick on Teviot, in 1856, the subject of it being a newly-run kipper-salmon, which turned the scales at thirty-two pounds. In landing him, I was indebted for assistance to a passer-by armed with a gaff-hook, and no doubt the duration of the run was greatly curtailed by this circumstance, the lower portion of my casting-line being made up of single gut. As it was, it took fully half an hour to master him. This was the largest salmon I ever caught. On the Floors Water, in November 1863, his Grace the Duke of Roxburghe having kindly invited me to enjoy a couple of days' fishing at a period when the river was well-stocked with large fish, I was successful in bringing to bank a splendidly-formed salmon of twenty-eight pounds, and, on the same day, another of twenty-two pounds. Having strong tackle and a trusty rod, I managed, with the assistance of Mr Stevenson, his Grace's head fisherman, who handled the punt and landing-net, to compass the capture of the larger fish in less than a quarter of an hour; but the water being large, he was evidently out of his beat, and in consequence succumbed quicker than a salmon of that size, acquainted with the rocky underlie would have done, for there is no doubt that a thorough knowledge of its position, and every surrounding advantage, operates greatly in increasing the resistance, and calling into play the strategic resources of the fish. My second day's sport that year, on the same stretch of river, embraced five salmon, averaging eighteen pounds each.

85. T T Stoddart 1866
Superior eating quality of perch

As an article of food the flesh of the perch is in good esteem – very superior to that of the carp, the tench, the bream, and the chub, and is held preferable by many to the flesh of the common trout. When in season, its firmness and curdy whiteness rival the same qualities as they are displayed in some of our most highly-prized salt-water fishes – the sole, for instance, and the red gurnard. One of the drawbacks to its more frequent appearance at the table, results from the supposed necessity, before cooking it, of removing the tough coat of scales and spinous fins with which, for defensive purposes, it is accoutred, – an operation, no doubt, which, when performed on a number of small-sized perch, involves a great deal of trouble. In the cooking of perch, however, be it known that the flaying operation is against all rule, and contrary to the practice of the experienced cook, whose aim it is, or ought to be, to keep intact the flavour of the fish, and preserve to it its juices and commendable properties. On Lentrathan Loch, and other famed perch-yielding expanses, it is considered barbarous to subject this fish to any other process, before brandering, than that of simply wiping it.

86. T T Stoddart 1866
Need to protect parr

T he good spirit, however, I am happy to observe, prevails in all the fishing clubs and associations – and these are now pretty numerous – established of late years on the banks of our Border rivers; for, as far as I can ascertain, they have unanimously set face against the taking of parrs, and small fry of every description. I feel at liberty to conclude, therefore, that the introduction of a clause into the General Fishery Act, making applicable to Tweed that portion of the Statute in question, which provides for the protection of the salmon fry in our northern rivers, so far from being objected to, by parties worth considering, will be hailed by them with great satisfaction. For my own part, I am quite satisfied it is high time that something should be done in the way of putting a stop to a practice, at once so unsportsmanlike, and so injurious to the salmon-fishings of Tweed and its tributaries. I have expressed decidedly, but not a whit too strongly, my views upon the treatment which the parr-stock of Tweed is receiving at the hands of a certain class of anglers. The amount of mischief annually inflicted on it from this source I may have underrated – exaggerated it I certainly have not. The disaster named, however, is only one of several to which the fry of our salmon lie exposed, and I have given it a prominent place in the list of casualties, not because it tells more severely than any of the others on the produce of the Tweed, but because it is capable to a much greater extent of being remedied.

87. H Stuart 1899
'Upwards of 200 lakes'

For my own part I have fished within the last fifteen years in upwards of 200 lakes that are not mere nameless tarns unsung in the prose, that is ever poetry of angling literature as written from week to week, but lakes of some repute. In these lakes I angled in six seasons alone on 279 days. It is obvious, therefore, that out of this great chain of lakes and this necessarily wide field of experiences, one must eliminate many lakes, and in the matter of experiences condescend only upon generalities that are universal, read and interpreted though 'specialities' that may be exceptions to the rules. With a view to limiting my remarks on lochs as homes for trout, and as waters giving them their characteristics as lake fish I may, therefore, confine myself to a selected few types.

88. H Stuart 1899
Poaching and a
close-time in Scotland

T he blessings of a close time cannot be over-estimated. From the absence of such a close time and the peculiar character of the Scottish law as to the right to take trout, the lakes and rivers of the country suffer to an incalculable degree. The personal, rather than the topographical, 'environment' of the poacher could easily be remedied, if our legislators could only be brought to see the immense moral and political influence angling is able to exercise over the community. The fishing rod is the best policeman, as Nottingham and Sheffield know, and Solomon were he now alive would alter his famous dictum 'Spare the rod and spoil the child' to 'Spare the rod and spoil the people.' In Scotland the absence of a close season conjoined with the fact that the right to take trout is a pertinent of the land has nowhere borne more baleful fruit than in the Orcadian lochs, which now hold very few trout compared with the immense numbers that used to jostle one another in the race of life in their bountiful waters. An Orcadian innkeeper lately wrote me a letter in which he stated that poaching was a thing of the past. As a matter of fact 'poaching' is only less rife, because there are fewer trout to 'poach,' if one can apply the term to men who as owners of a square foot of territory on a loch side have, in Scots Law, the right to fish all over its waters. A few years ago one could take baskets of from 33lb. to 40lb. on Loch Harray. Its deterioration began with the institution of poaching by set lines and nets, and has been steadily maintained. In one season a single Orcadian sent 1000lb. of trout to Billingsgate, and there are some hundreds of nets – the number is by some placed at 1000 – on this lake alone!

89. H Stuart 1899
The rainbow trout favoured

T he opponents of the rainbow trout have a two-fold objection to urge against its introduction into British waters. They allege (1) that: the fish is a cannibal of lusty appetite, whose primest condition is contemporaneous with the spawning time of our common trout; and (2) that the fish is of such strongly marked migratory habits that it disappears from all streams in which it is placed if any road of escape is left open to it, whether to the sea or to the more confined waters of lakes to which the streams are tributary. It is, of course, obvious that these pleas are what lawyers term alternative, and are not, therefore, necessarily contradictory. At the same time, it may be pointed out that if the fish do not take up their permanent abode in streams from which they can escape to the sea or elsewhere, their introduction into such streams is a perfectly safe experiment, for the injury they can do to the nature front must be as evanescent and passing as their cohabitation with them.

90. H Stuart 1899
The importance of a good boat

A t the same time every little counts in angling, and it is just as important that the loch angler should secure, if possible, the best type of boat suitable for his purpose, as it is that he should use the flies most suitable for the water he is fishing.

It may here be stated, that for reasons which a subsequent chapter will reveal, two anglers should never fish from the same boat save under the most exceptional circumstances, and hence there is no necessity that a boat for loch fishing should be large, provided it is seaworthy, of sufficient beam and depth to be stable, and is otherwise sufficiently roomy to give greater freedom of movement than the limitation to 'coughing and sneezing' implies.

Presuming that the loch fisher from a boat fishes alone the proper length of boat is one of some twelve feet. It should be sufficiently light to be easily rowed, turned, and generally manoeuvred and transported from loch to loch, and yet, at the same time, as already stated, of sufficient beam to be steady, and of sufficient strength to resist not only the buffets of the deep, but what is more important, the frequent and generally unexpected impact with sunken rocks and gravel banks.

91. H Stuart 1899
Flies, fished deep and shallow

T he value in use of such a division becomes clear when one considers that it secures a classification for angling purposes of flies that may and should be used as 'first dropper,' or 'bob' flies, flies, that is to say, that can be fished high, and flies, that are second, third, or tail flies, which may and should be fished deep. It may be observed that the sensational theory of the fly in its practical application really amounts to the laying down of the axiom that the more natural or imitative a fly is, and the more natural the manner in which it is brought under the notice of a trout, the less likely is that trout to be alarmed by the necessary discrepancy between the appearance and movements of the most cunningly contrived and cleverly presented imitation and the real Simon Pure. This is the general principle underlying the theory which admits, in accordance with the irresistible deductions drawn from angling experience, that trout take and always have taken imitations of 'flies that fly,' made to behave in a manner in which they never do behave or, in other words, in a most unnatural manner. Dead flies or half drowned flies do not swim up stream or sail either in the eye or close to the wind in a lake, but nevertheless we know that both in streams and lochs trout take our winged messengers of death, whose vitality thus displays itself in a triumph over the grave.

92. H Stuart 1899
Insists on small flies

P ersonally I never use a fly dressed on a hook above No. 12 on the Limerick scale, and cannot conceive why any larger hook should be used for ordinary trout, unless, of course, one is compelled to imitate a large natural fly, in which case necessity justifies the abuse. If salmon will occasionally take trout flies when they reject salmon flies; if the largest fish in our rivers feed on 'smuts,' mere pin points incapable of human imitation, even when dressed on a 000 hook, and big sea-trout will take finely dressed flies on No. 14 hooks, it is obvious that the trout one can reasonably expect to catch in the majority of our lakes do not need a large fly and are, in fact, usually angled for with flies that are too large. I presume that many anglers regard not merely the 'raising' but also the 'holding' power of hooks as a determining factor in the size of the fly to be used, but again I reply that if I can kill 3 trout weighing 18½lbs. in 38½ minutes of actual fishing in a loch in a dead calm casting over rising fish with flies on No. 13 hooks, it is obvious that there is not much amiss with their holding power, especially as one of those fish happened to be a 10lb fish. And even if there were, it is clear that if sport is to be determined by the difficulties overcome and by the handicap allowance the angler is willing to give the fish, then the smaller the fly and the finer the tackle the greater is the sport.

93. H Stuart 1899
Timing the strike

After one or two failures I, at last, secured just the sort of rise desired. The fish, apparently one of the normal weight of the trout in the lake (1½ lbs.), came deliberately up to the fly, his head being towards it and towards the boat. He turned as he took the fly and went almost straight down. The line was nearly taut, and I had the greatest possible difficulty in keeping the old angling Adam from yielding to the temptation. I succeeded, however, in restraining this legacy of another bite, with the result that when the fish had sunk some three feet down, he opened his oracular jaws, shot the fly out with great force, and presented me not only with an exception to the golden rule of the happy mean in striking which I had endeavoured to cultivate, but also with a very interesting and instructive lesson in the often unsuspected and unnoted means of defence against our guile in which Nature has thought fit to panoply her cold-blooded children. There was no question here as to how the fish was holding the fly. It had disappeared and his mouth was closed. Whenever he felt what a very bony and insipid member of the insect race he had secured, he rejected it.

94. H Stuart 1899
Dry fly may have its uses on canals

Another matter which may fairly be claimed to fall within my subject is the question of fly-fishing in canals. I am not in a position to quote statistics but to judge from casual experience the number of canals in this country which hold trout must be very limited. No doubt there are few or no canals in some of whose reaches an occasional trout is not to be found, but on the whole trout are not so common in canals as they might be, considering the by no means insuperable objections which may be urged against the stocking of these waterways with trout. The principal of these objections no doubt is the very considerable poaching which prevails amongst bargemen. For the most part the water of our canals is pure enough to carry trout, while as many of them are fished by ticket, there is no reason, even when allowance is made for the higher temptation, why poaching should be more rife amongst the trout than amongst the coarse fish which are the usual objects of the canal angler's quest. Apart from poaching, there are many canals which could carry a fair head of trout, and if our friends the rainbows and fontinales have ultimately a verdict 'for doom' pronounced against them, our canals would be the very places to stock with the large surplus population of these fish, thrown by reason of their condemnation on the fish farmer's hands.

Fly fishing in a canal, either with or without a breeze, would be precisely the same as loch fishing. On canals, moreover, one could more readily use the dry-fly than on lochs. In the latter the total absence of any current takes away from dry-fly fishing one of its essentials, for on still water a fly only floats, it does not float down, and to drag it is to risk a departure from nature. In a gentle breeze in a loch, you can make a dry fly travel with the wind, and to a certain extent can therefore imitate a fly being carried on the surface. This method is really 'dapping.' In fact in loch fishing, save at the mouths

LOCHS AND LOCH FISHING,

BY

HAMISH STUART, M.A., LL.B.

"But the luxurious angler admires another concert. He loves no musick, but the twang of the line; nor any sound, save the ecchoes of waters; no rest nor pause, but impatient till they bite; no flats, nor sharps, but solitary pools and rapid streams; no beats nor shakes, but struggling and strangling; and, in short, no close except that of the pannier. So that I may properly call his harmony their haltering. . . . . Here's suitable diversion, our exercise has equaliz'd the ballance of success: Not an artist amongst us barren of sport. Nor the water out of temper. . . . . We may flatter ourselves the town's our own."—"*Northern Memoirs," by Richard Franck (1624—1690).*

"What though, like commoners of air
We wander out, we know not where,
But either house or hall;
Yet nature's charms—the hills and woods,
The sweeping vales and foaming floods—
Are free alike to all."—*Burns.*

"Why, ye tenants of the lake
For me your watery haunts forsake?
. . . . . .
Common friends to you and me,
Nature's gifts to all are free."—*Id.*

LONDON:
CHAPMAN & HALL, LIMITED.
SCARBOROUGH:
"THE ANGLER" OFFICE, ST. NICHOLAS STREET.
1899.

of burns, you can only use a dry fly by casting it 'very dry' beside a rising trout and letting it float for a second or two motionless. If the trout takes it, you can catch him with a dry fly, but you do not take him by dry fly fishing in the strict sense. I have always found a very small wet fly, fished far and fine and well sunk, far more deadly than the dry-fly or even a floating May-fly, when that is 'up.' In a canal it would however, be more often feasible to fish dry-fly, because there is often sufficient current to float it along in a natural kind of way.

95. T Thornton 1896
The great perch from Loch Lomond

I n our way, passed through the straits of Loch Lomond, a most likely place for pike: still we had no rise, when, in turning gently round a dark bay, I felt a fish strike, and ordered the boat to stop: I perceived that my bait had sunk deep, but not recollecting the additional force the fish acquired thereby, imagined him to be of great magnitude. My tackle was not to be surpassed, I had plenty of water to work him, and no trees or roots to trouble me, but he made the rod, at every exertion, bend to the water. After much trouble he was secured in the landing-net, and proved to be a perch of about seven pounds and a half. I never saw so fine a fed fellow, and what had given him additional powers, and had deceived me, was, as I found, his being hooked by the belly part, which gave him the full strength of his head and tail. Fish so hooked have deceived me, and no doubt many brother anglers before.

The landlord at Luss, in our absence, had exerted all his talents to render everything as comfortable as possible, and the servants expressed themselves much better pleased with the accommodations for their horses, etc., than they were the preceding evening. Got the portable stilliards to weigh my perch, about which there were various conjectures. Mr G. guessed he might be under eight pounds; Mr P. thought he might be more. His precise weight, however, was seven pounds three ounces, or thereabouts. He was very thick about the shoulders, and I regret I did not measure him, as I never saw a fish so well fed.

96. T Thornton 1896
Big trout from Loch Tay

T he breeze now increased; Mr P. had not had one rise; but, on steering round a bank, which projected into the lake, he hooked a fish at almost every instant, killed several, and at length secured one which required all our assistance to land, and which might weigh about five pounds. I now began to hope for good sport; my bait was so large that I thought none but a trout or salmon would attempt it, for no other fish, we were told, were to be found in this part of the lake. Mr P., whose flies I had changed, putting on my favourite black fly, caught several good fish, and I hooked one which soon convinced me he meant to try the strength of my tackle. We were obliged to bring to, and I landed him with great difficulty, being but slightly hooked: he was a noble fellow, and we estimated him at nine pounds. I afterwards had very good sport with two large trout, not quite so big as this; and, trolling with a bait of near half a pound, expected to kill a trout of fifteen pounds at least, the boatman solemnly affirming that such were frequently caught. However, I landed without another rise; but such a weight of fine fish I never saw taken in one day; and the boatman, whom I found to be Lord Breadalbane's fisherman, and from using his nets constantly might be supposed to know the nature and size of the fish in this lake, declared that there never had been so many, or so fine, taken in it in any day before.

97. E M Tod 1903
Dry fly has some uses in Scotland

I n the writer's opinion, the dry fly is neither more nor less than the slow and gradual evolution of its projenitor the wet fly, adapted to rivers which are specially suitable.

The more we fish, the more do trout become educated and knowing; and whether it be in Scotland or elsewhere, when trout are few and far between, or many, but knowing to a degree; the tendency will be for men who have tried all they know with the wet fly, to take a leaf out of one's neighbour's book, and try what the dry fly will do on occasion.

Let me be very clear about this, however, lest I may be misunderstood.

I have no patience whatever with the extreme purist of the dry fly, who, in the month of April or beginning of May would not unbend by a hair's breadth, were he placed on the Deveron or any such Scottish river.

At present, I should advise the southern angler who comes to fish in Scotland, to let the dry fly be 'his crutch rather than his staff,' on the majority of our rivers; and especially in the early spring.

98. E M Tod 1903
The wet fly ever up-stream

And now fish the centre current, moving up gradually, till you near the rapid, or rapids, descending from the pool or stream above. All such rapids must be fished up, and the line should be short, especially if the angler is wading in fairly deep water, and below the trout, of course. Throw *up*, with a quick, direct, forcible cast, and then, lower the point of the rod, so that, when the line is thrown, your rod points up the stream, and is quite close to the surface of the river; rod and line, for one brief second, forming one unbroken extension pointing directly up-stream. In this way – and in this alone – you command your fly from the moment it alights; and you will find that, even then, you have to raise the point of your rod overhead, or sideways, with considerable rapidity, as your flies often come towards you, at a great pace. And, here, it is necessary to dwell a little on the proper fishing up-stream of any rapid like this. One throw is no real test. You must throw again and again, the oftener the better, in a given time; four, five, or six rapid casts with a short line, and then, if you like, try the water on either side. But remember, when fishing a narrow 'throat' up, if the fly halts for a moment, look out; for it means a trout, and you must tighten on him instantly, and pull him down stream gently – if you can do so.

99. E M Tod 1903
The perfect rod

T he rod most suited to any particular fisherman is largely a matter of taste. Some men prefer a two-handed trout rod for a large river. I have a very excellent rod of fourteen feet, and I seldom use it. So much for taste. But, it is not what I have done, or *do*, for I may be often wrong, and doubtless am often mistaken; but, when I see how invariably the best fly-fishermen take to a rod which they can use easily with one hand, I am strengthened in my faith in such rods.

As for its length, that is a matter of wrist power and daily use; but 10½ to 11½ feet is a useful length for the fly rod on a large river. A great deal of excellent work can be done with one of 10½ or 11 feet, as I can testify, provided that the rod be powerful enough to lift a long line 'clean' off the water, without which the rod has no real backbone. People do not sufficiently realize that lifting the line 'clane an' cliver' off the water is the first great essential to any well-delivered cast. If the line at the lifting gets 'drowned,' the forward throw will prove a failure.

It is here that so many cheap, ready-made shop rods fail utterly; they are mere toys, unless they possess power. And I hold that the perfection of a rod reads, *Backbone plus delicacy*, and that delicacy is a delusion minus 'backbone.'

100. E M Tod 1903
Wet flies should be wet

I shall take away the breath of some purist anglers when I say that, often when I wish my fly to sink one or two inches as soon as thrown, I deliberately take the wings and hackle between the fore-finger and thumb of my right hand, and, having wet my fingers well, rub the feathers thoroughly.

Especially has this discovery of mine been found to be useful, in fine and calm weather, when the smallest midge-flies, 'doubles' or even 'singles,' were to the front. If the learner will take a fly, and place it dry in a tumbler of water, he will find that it is largely kept from sinking by reason of air-bells. The wings look as if they were coated with a thin layer of glass, whilst small bells get entangled amongst the fibres of the hackle. These air-bubbles, I am certain, often make the trout needlessly suspicious of a wet fly. The bubbles get completely rubbed out, partly because the wet finger and thumb, thus deprive the feathers of their natural oil. Be that as it may, I boldly avow that when I have observed trout shyly regarding small midgeflies, newly put on, I have rubbed the feathers well with wetted finger and thumb, and have begun to basket them rapidly immediately afterwards.

101. E M Tod 1903
Slowly and quietly upstream

He, of course, knew how to cast and how to place his fly – very few better.

When trout are feeding on the surface: (1) wade gently; (2) make each cast a true one; (3) cast up and across (at times straight up); (4) don't sink your flies more than you can help, because trout at present are expecting to see the natural insect floating down with gauzy wings erect on the surface; (5) cast repeatedly, and when a trout takes the fly, tighten the line instantly rather than 'strike:' then up with the point of the rod and get command of your trout as soon as you can; (6) finally, net him, if possible, just where you are standing, in the water. Methodically continue to search the hang step by step across the river, and back again, till you have fished it completely out.

Use two or even three flies. I prefer two flies placed six feet apart, when I am fishing in a dead calm, or wherever trout are over-fished, to the usual three flies one yard apart; but I use, at times, only one.

102. E M Tod 1903
Reels and 'smashes'

And now as to reels. Let me remark that I prefer gun-metal and brass-bronzed reels to all others. Vulcanite reels break, if they happen to fall upon a stone; and I know nothing to the advantage of aluminium, save lightness. There are many patented reels about: of which the 'Moscrop,' seems to be a good sample.

I do not desire a reel to be excessively light, since it helps to balance the rod, placed as it is *behind* the 'grip,' not in front of it, as of old: and I regard as unnecessary, many of the so-called improvements in reels. My own opinion is, that the very best quality of brass or gun-metal 'check' reels with revolving plates, are hard to beat. To give them a fair chance, they should frequently be taken to pieces, the plate removed, the interior thoroughly cleansed, and the spindle delicately oiled. If this is not done, the sand works its way in under the revolving plate, and will wear the reel out, long before its time.

How often does it occur that some angling friend will confide in you how frequently he gets 'smashed up,' especially when fishing a large and somewhat rapid river. Let us suppose a case! The angler is casting up stream, in the teeth of the breeze, and is using very fine-drawn gut. The force needed to cast the fine gut line necessitates the point of the rod often coming very near the water, and now and then, even touching it. As the line alights, a large trout seizes the fly and makes a wild dash for liberty. Then follows a heavy pull with the inevitable smash.

103. E M Tod 1903
Three trout at a time, but precariously

I once landed three half-pound trout (on the Cumberland Eden), one on each fly; and this when I dared not take a step, so fearfully slippery was the wading, and so strong the current. Yet I basketed all three, without moving an inch from the spot, to the delight of the keeper, who watched me the whole time, and waved his hat to cheer me, as he knew that I could hear nothing, wading in that turmoil of rushing water. And when I had all three safely in the creel, it was a veritable triumph of my system, for I was able to kill each trout (and basket it) quite easily and with certainty, and was (without a minute's delay) fishing again as if nothing had happened. Yet such was the wading, that I had to use a spike on my landing-net handle, and make quite sure of each foot being firmly planted, ere I dared to lift the other.

I was not sorry to leave that place and go to a safer – but not till I had fished it thoroughly.

104. E M Tod 1903
'Wee doubles' promoted

W hile I was resident in England, where I have spent nearly thirty years of my life, one way and another, Mr John Forrest, fishing-tackle maker, of 24, Thomas Street, Grosvenor Square, London, W., in writing to me, once remarked that he was beginning to sell these 'doubles' very well, even in the south. But, he added, that English customers had expressed the wish that they could be also had, as eyed hooks.

Now, such tiny delicate hooks brazed together, would prove in actual practice, a complete failure, for reasons too many to explain *in extenso*.

His letter set me thinking, and I sent him up a very simple little invention to meet the needs of these eyed-fly fishermen.

It consists of one eyed hook whipped to an ordinary 'blind' hook of the same size, and Mr Forrest took to it at once. When finished, the flies look, what they really are; quite a little success.

Above all things, these small 'doubles' must be movable, else, when one of the hooks gets fixed in the upper jaw and the other hook in the lower jaw, they would frequently snap. As they are held together, however, only by the silk thread, there is a great deal of 'give and take;' and this saves the situation. I seldom find them break.

105. D Webster 1885
A long, spliced rod

*T**he Rod.* – The trouting-rod which I am in the habit of using is a two-handed spliced rod, measuring from 13 feet 6 inches to 13 feet 8 inches. It consists of three pieces. The butt is made of ash, the middle piece of hickory, and the top of lancewood. When greater lightness is desired, lime-tree may be used for the butt: what the rod gains in this respect, however, is lost in durability. Attached to the extremity of the top piece is a strong loop of twisted horse-hair, through which is passed the loop of the hair-line used in casting. If the rod be well balanced, nicely tapered, and neatly and firmly tied together, its sweep and action in casting will be smooth and even throughout its entire length. But it is as well to have the middle piece somewhat stiff when one is using the loopline. For undue suppleness in a rod – and in the middle piece lies the test – is just as fatal to good casting as too great rigidity. A spliced rod of this kind is much lighter than the ordinary brass-jointed rod, and casts a much better line.

106. D Webster 1885
Tapered horse-hair line

*T*he *Casting-Line.* – This line is made of horse-hairs, not too firmly twisted – the lengths of hairs being knotted at their junction, and the ends neatly tied with well-rosined silk thread. It tapers gradually from the loop to the gut. The number of hairs composing the thickest part of the line at the loop ranges from thirty-six to forty-five, according to fineness, diminishing gradually to five or six at the point where the gut-line is attached. The length of the casting-line should be from 18 to 20 feet. The loop at the top is about three inches long, and is passed through the corresponding loop of smaller size attached to the rod.

The Gut-Line. – The gut-line, as distinguished from the casting-line proper, measures from 16 to 17 feet, and so the total length of line from the loop to the trail-fly is from 34 to 37 feet. The gut should be tapered as well as the hair-line – the strongest lengths being selected for the portion next the casting-line, and the finer for the remainder, so as to preserve the tapering of the line throughout its entire length from loop to fly.

107. D Webster 1885
Accurate casting with the 'strap'

S
o far as mere facility in casting is concerned, the loop-line possesses a marked advantage over the ordinary line in rendering the angler much more independent of the assistance of the wind, and much less impeded by its opposition. The greater weight and consequent momentum of his line enable him to cast his flies to within a few points of the wind if necessary, where, with a lighter line, much good water might be lost, and much time spent in crossing and re-crossing to get a favouring breeze; while in the entire absence of wind he can take full advantage of the great length of his line, and cast with unerring precision. Unless in exceptional circumstances of wind and weather, the angler with the loop-line ought to be able to lay his flies on the water within a few inches of any given point – and this, too, from a distance of 40 or 50 feet. The value of such a cast in clear water can scarcely be overestimated, especially when it is remembered that the line carries three times as many flies as the advocates of the short-line system use when fishing up-stream. Every part of the river may thus be most favourably and easily reached without the necessity of deep wading, and the concomitant evil of unduly disturbing the water.

108. D Webster 1885
Always fish up-stream

Lastly, as the fish all lie with their heads up-stream, the angler who fishes up-stream approaches them from behind, and is consequently outside the range of their vision. To fish down in clear water brings him more under the observation of the trout, and thereby lessens his chance of catching them; for if a fish get but a glimpse of the fisher, it will require more than a deftly cast fly to reassure it that all's well. Of course the angler is more conspicuous on the bank than when wading; but even in the latter case, he should remember that the sharp eye of the fish serves it well, not only by direct vision to see the angler's feet in its own element, but also, through the influence of refraction, to discern strange appearances above it. In a black water the trout cannot, of course, see so well, and in that case the angler may fish down with less risk of being observed.

The reason why so many anglers prefer to fish down in all conditions of water is simply that they find it easier to do so. And no doubt fishing upstream is more difficult than fishing down. Even if we take no account of the greater physical exertion required to wade against the current, successful up-stream fishing implies more knowledge of the habits and habitats of the fish, more nicety and precision in casting, greater dexterity in managing the line when cast and in bringing it properly home, a quicker eye in detecting a rise, and a readier hand in responding thereto.

109. D Webster 1885
How to cast

I n casting, the rod should be grasped with both hands – the left near the butt, and the right about eight or nine inches higher up. There being no reel on the rod, the hands can be so placed as to secure the amount of leverage necessary for a good cast. The upper parts of the arms are kept close to the body, and only the wrists and forearms are brought into play; so that anything like 'thrashing' the water is avoided. Having made his first cast over the water mainly to get his line out in front of him, the young angler must now raise the point of his rod a little to bring the line round in a curve sufficiently near him, and so much under command as will enable him to lift it gently from the water and to make the next cast. This movement is effected by raising the rod gradually towards the perpendicular, and causing the point of it to describe something of a horse-shoe curve, when the line will be brought gently round in a corresponding sweep overhead, and derive, from this motion and its own weight, sufficient momentum to urge it forward to its full length. The point of the rod should not be carried much behind the body, and the line should not be sent out to its full length behind, but brought round in a curve, following the motion of the rod until fairly on the forward movement, when a slightly quickened action is imparted, and the rod is brought nearly to the horizontal. The line is thus gradually straightened in its forward course until it measures its full length over the stream – first touching the water near the middle point of the hair-line, when the droppers will fall gently, and almost simultaneously, with the trail-fly.

110. D Webster 1885
Worming the burn, up-stream

He may capture sufficient to satisfy his ambition, and more than fill his creel. He will find that the earlier hours of the day are the best; the 'takes' are fewer after one or two o'clock in the afternoon; but it is no uncommon occurrence for twelve or eighteen dozen to be picked up before that time in a well-stocked burn. A day's 'take' of burn-trout looks better when stated in dozens than in pounds. They are more numerous than large; and as they generally pay promptly for what they get, and are rarely credited with a worm, the angler must be content to conduct this branch of his 'silent business' on the admirable principle of 'small profits and quick returns.'

If the water be clear, the angler must of course fish up. Using an ordinary trout-rod and a short fine line, a small Stewart tackle, and a tiny lively worm, let him drop his bait gently into the pools or into the streams, behind stones and below banks, in ripples and in eddies, remembering that wherever there is sufficient – and sometimes even where there is scarcely sufficient – water to cover a fish, the chances are that he may raise one. But he must keep well out of sight, and take care lest his own shadow or that of his rod fall athwart the stream.

111. D Webster 1885
Grayling held in contempt

Mr Blaine's opinion is that 'the grayling is an inanimate fish when hooked.' Even 'Ephemera,' who acknowledges that the grayling is 'a favourite fish' of his, is constrained to admit that 'it takes a fly boldly, but does not show much boldness after having taken it and been hooked;' and that though 'it is a gamesome fish, it is not a game one.' To capture a brace of such creatures may by some of our Southern friends be esteemed a fine art and gentle; but, pray, let all anglers who are also sportsmen reserve, if possible, their tackle and their talent for a worthier fish.

Some consideration might be shown for the grayling if it possessed even that secondary qualification of a good fish – the power to evoke pleasurable anticipations when there rings out

'That tocsin of the soul, the dinner-bell.'

Tastes differ, and there may be grayling and grayling; but if I am to judge from those that I have tried – and they were in their best season – grayling are not to be named in the same breath with the most ordinary trout. Walton reminds us that Gesner says, 'the French value him so highly that they say he feeds on gold;' but what of that, if the French of his day were as discriminating as those in ours who prefer bull-trout to salmon? In spite of all that is said of its 'thymy' and its 'cucumber' fragrance, and its 'firm and flaky flesh,' I consider even the much-derided pike immeasurably its superior in edible virtues. Walton says that 'all that write of the umber (grayling) declare him very medicinable.' Possibly – and, judging by his flavour, very probably; but if so, let him be treated as medicine and used as sparingly.

112. J Wilson 1840
Fishing the shore of the loch

I f you have no boat, you had better fish from the shore. Some people (Professor Wilson, for example) prefer doing so, whether they have a boat or not; and if you don't desire to keep your feet particularly dry (in which case you had better also keep your room for a few days), you must wade – sometimes to a considerable actual depth, if you are a tall bold man, or to a proportional apparent depth, if you are a short shy one. A young bachelor may, of course, wade deeper than a married man, of the same dimensions, who has a wife and family.

In fishing from shore, try to get the wind behind you, and – at least if you have that object in view, – don't fish on the lee-side of the loch. When you have waded in as far as you feel inclined, and supposing the wind to blow either directly or diagonally from the shore, say into your right ear when your face is lake-ward, then take a few casts before you, and rather to the right hand, bringing your flies across and somewhat down the wind, then stretch out with a more lengthened throw directly forward, then sweep away, cast after cast, to the left, taking always two or three throws in every radius in a straight line with each other, beginning with the shorter and ending with the more extended stretch. Always complete your semicircle by casting quite in shore, almost in a line, though slightly in advance, from where you entered; for, if the place is good, the very ground on which you stand, may be a favourite haunt for food or play. Then take a step or two onwards, and recommence again from right to left, or *vice versa*, as your case may be – for if the wind, that fickle element, chops about, you must also act the weather-cock, and change your tactics.

113. J Younger 1864
Flies emerge from maggots

Before proceeding to give my selection of trout flies, I would wish to observe how these flies are bred, and the successive appearances they present in their change from one state to another, which will assist you to account upon philosophical principles for various phenomena occurrent in angling, which tend to confuse the ideas of superficial observers.

If in the middle of winter you lift a stone from the bottom of the river, you may perceive on the under side of it numbers of small cases, formed of mud-particles, cemented by a glutinous substance into a consistency like brown paper; by pressing this case you will see that it contains a dark green maggot, or chrysalis of the future water-fly. These are in myriads, and constitute a portion of the food of trouts throughout the winter, as they do in their more fully developed state when winged in the summer. On 23d November, 1837, from the stomach of a trout about half-a-pound weight, I counted out three hundred of these maggots all in the skins, many of them still retaining the appearance of life.

114. J Younger 1864
Always upstream for trout

W hen in bright weather and clear unruffled water you cannot succeed in throwing your flies across, or rather at a considerable angle upwards, and letting them swim down of their own accord, with no visible pull upon them, then turn your face up the water, and whether in stream or smooth pool, there throw straight up, or at such slight angle from straight up as circumstances of depth or other impediment may permit. In this way, your fly falling lightly above the feeding trout, he is apt to snap it the instant it alights; your quick acknowledgment of feeling him being down against his mouth and body, he can hardly miss being hooked; then lead him gently down towards you, which action alarms none above. Then proceed a step upwards, and in the next throw, breaking new water, you have a new chance.

It is easy to conceive how readily a trout is hooked in this way; for when the fine gut is wet and pliant, the moment the fly is dropped on the surface the action of the water folds it inwards, bringing it to the trout's mouth like a natural fly afloat, and not seemingly held as hanging against the current. It is thus slack when he sucks it in, and you have only to give the slightest pull, which, being against him, gives advantage to get such a hold as settles his concern with existence. In the common way, fishing from above, the thing appears to the trout out of course, and this he perceives, from an instinct, more quickly than Sir Humphry Davy could have reasoned it from his best philosophy and knowledge of angling. Indeed, in fishing downwards in thin clear water with flies hanging against the stream, it is a wonder one should get a rise of a trout at all.

115. J Younger 1864
A large, two-handed rod

With a rod of about fourteen feet, large enough for having command of water, even when fishing in the Tweed, you will also have most success in these small streams; as with a rod well balanced, of equal spring from hand to top, and a casting line of suitable weight, you will throw to the point you wish with ease and softness – and walking upright, like the 'Lord of the Isles,' disdain to crouch or hide. Thus, too, by throwing out only half the length of line you could do if necessary, you will in small streams nip the trout up as he rises, and be more successful by open means than by hidlins; and why bind to fish with one hand only? If you have two hands left from the Crimean or Indian wars, use both, except when you require to scratch your lug. Thus make your angling easy, pleasurable, and man-like. The balance of rod should be thus – when you hold it by the butt, in a horizontal position, it should not droop in the top, though on the point of doing so; and it is an observable fact, that a well-balanced rod, always feels one half lighter in the hand than an ill-balanced one, although both of the same weight, upon the whole, if weighed in scales. This occurs from being top-heavy, or too yielding in the middle, where it should stand stiffest, yielding rather more both below and above the centre. I approve also of the extreme top for two, or not exceeding three, inches being very pliant, such as whalebone rendered finely small will make it; as in fishing on the stream-water.

116. J Younger 1864
A big, spliced rod preferred

E ven for travelling, I would prefer tied joints, as, wherever a person has time to stop and fish, though only for a day or two, he has at least five minutes to spare for tying up his rod in a sufficient manner.

Rods are often breaking at brass joints, and those who use them, instead of bringing in a back-load of fish, are often arriving home from the water telling you, 'I've broke my rod!' Such sickening news may generally be prevented by tied joints.

A one-hand trout rod, between thirteen and fourteen feet long, is very convenient and pleasant to use, even when wading deep in the Tweed. But in moderate wading, we cannot command much water with a rod of less than fifteen or sixteen feet. I would recommend that a rod be made soft and pliable for about three inches on the top, much more so than is generally done, as a hard springy maintop readily twitches the hook from the trout's mouth.

'Tighten' rather than 'strike'

H ence, throwing the line for trout does not require the same regularity of plan and manner as the casting for salmon, since it is often more necessary to throw aslant, upwards, or straight across, than downwards. And, indeed, in trout angling generally, it is very improper to hang the fly on the stream, far more so to pull against it, as the natural fly never floats in that direction.

In fishing either stream or pool regularly over, cast the fly across, or slant it considerably upwards, and let it float down the current of its own accord till it come gradually full round, managing your rod so as all the while to keep the line and flies under such command, that should a trout touch the hook unseen below the water, you can detect him on the instant. This action is simply a *tightening feel*, as the trout is generally previously hooked from the natural resistance of the floating line. If he is not felt to be hooked, then it is necessary to pull full up and make another throw; but never let the first pull in feeling for a trout be so decidedly forcible as to be called a *strike*, for it ought not to be done with a third part of the force requisite to lift the line clear off the surface, as is necessary when making another throw. Indeed, in casting generally for either salmon or trout, the angler should never snatch his line quickly from the water, but give it first a gentle pull, and let the lifting it be a second and brisker action; as a large trout, or sometimes a salmon, may be following the fly, and may readily, at that particular instant, be just seizing it.

Bibliography

Aflalo, Frederick George (ed.), *A Book of Fishing Stories.* London and New York, 1913.

Anderson, John, *Autumn Gleanings or Ears of Barley.* Edinburgh and Perth, 1885.

Anonymous, *Songs of the Edinburgh Angling Club.* Edinburgh, 1858, 1878.

Anonymous (Tait, J), *Angler's Guide for the Shetlands.* Lerwick, 1903.

Bantock, W, *The Lochs and Rivers of Sutherland.* In *Manchester Angler's Association,* 1880, 1, pp. 138–171.

Bark, Conrad Voss, *A History of Fly Fishing.* Ludlow, 1992.

Begg, Robert Burns, *The Loch Leven Angler.* Edinburgh and Glasgow, 1874, 1934.(2nd edition with foreword by Thomas Burns-Begg, revised by John Johnstone.)

Bertram, James G ('Ellangowan'), *The Border Angler: a Guide to the Tweed and its Tributaries.* Edinburgh and London, 1858 and later n.d.

Bickerdyke, John (see Cook, C H)

Biggart, David A, *The Scottish National Angling Club Associations, 1880–1980.* Glasgow (privately published), 1979.

'Black Palmer' (identity unknown), *Scotch Loch Fishing.* Edinburgh, 1882.

Blakey, Robert ('Palmer Hackle'), *The Angler's Guide to the Rivers and Lochs of Scotland.* London, Edinburgh and Glasgow, 1854; 1859.

Angling or How to Angle and Where to Go. London, 1854, 1857, 1871, 1880, 1898.

Hints on Angling with Suggestions for Angling Excursions . . . Irish Waters. London, 1846.

Historical Sketches of the Angling of All Nations. London, 1856.

Old Faces in New Masks. London, 1859.

'Borderer' (see Brown, William, Sorley)

Bradley, Arthur G, *Clear Waters. Trouting Days and Trouting Ways in Wales, the West Country and the Scottish Borderland.* London, 1915.

Braithwaite, Cecil, *Fishing Vignettes. Being Extracts from a Diary and Other Fragments, 1875–1922.* London, 1923.

Braithwaite, George F, *The Salmonidae of Westmoreland, Angling Reminiscences and Leaves from an Angler's Notebook.* Kendal, 1884.

Brander, Michael, *Soho for the Colonel. On the Trail of Colonel Thornton.* London, 1961.

A Hunt Around the Highlands. Saul, Glos., USA, 1973 (reprint of preceding).

Bridgett, Robert Currie, *Dry Fly Fishing.* London, 1922, 1929.
    By Loch and Stream. Angling Sketches. London, 1922, 1928.
    Loch Fishing in Theory and Practice. London, 1924, 1926, 1962.
    Tight Lines. Angling Sketches. London, 1926.
    See Trout Fishing. London 1929.
Briggs, Ernest E, *Angling and Art in Scotland.* London, 1908.
Brown, J A Harvie (see Harvie-Brown, J A)
Brown, James Moray, *Stray Sport.* Edinburgh and London, 1893, 2 vols.
Brown, William, *The Natural History of the Salmon as Ascertained by Recent Experiments at Stormontfield.* Glasgow, 1862.
Brown, William Sorley ('Rainbow', 'Borderer') *Secrets of Border Angling.* Galashiels, 1907.
    The Ne'er-Do-Weel. Some Waterside Sketches. Galshiels, 1909.
Burns Begg, R (see Begg, R B)
Cairncross, David, *The Origins of the Silver Eel, with Remarks on Bait and Fly Fishing.* London, 1862.
Calderwood, William L, *The Salmon Rivers and Lochs of Scotland.* London, 1909, 1921.
    Salmon and Sea Trout. London, 1930.
    Salmon! Experiences and Reflections. London, 1938.
Carroll, William, *The Angler's Vade Mecum . . . and Where Found.* Edinburgh, 1818.
Chaytor, Alfred H, *Letters to a Salmon Fisher's Sons.* London, 1910, 1919, 1925.
Chrystal, Robert A, *Angling Theories and Methods.* London, 1927.
    Angling at Lochboisdale, South Uist. Notes on an Angling Journal, 1882–1937. London, 1939.
Clarke, Capt., *Angler's Desideratum . . . Half a Century.* Edinburgh, 1839.
Cole, C W and Ralston, W, *Messrs Kamdene, Barnsburie and D'Alston's Tour in the North.* London, Edinburgh and Glasgow, n.d. (1898).
Coleby, Ronald J W, *Regional Angling Literature. A Check List of Books on Angling and the Salmon Fisheries in Scotland, Northern England, Wales and Ireland.* Lincoln, 1979.
Colquhoun, John, *Rocks and Rivers.* London, 1849.
    Salmon Casts and Stray Shots. Edinburgh, 1858.
    Sporting Days. Edinburgh and London, 1866.
    The Moor and the Loch. Edinburgh, 1840, 1841, 1851, 1878, 1880, 1884, 1888 (under diverse titles).
Conway, James (see Walter, J C)
Cook, Charles H ('John Bickerdyke'), *Days in Thule with Rod, Gun and Camera.* London, 1894, 1897.
Courtney Williams, A, *Angling Diversions.* London, 1945.
Crombie, Benjamin W, *Modern Athenians.* Edinburgh, 1882 (2 vols).
Davy, Sir Humphry, *Salmonia or Days of Fly Fishing in a Series of Conversations.* London, 1828, 1829, 1832, 1851.
Dawson, William, *Dawson's Illustrated Guide to the Borderland, including*

the Angler's Notebook for the Tweed . . . and Wansbeck. Berwick-upon-Tweed, 1885 (and later under various titles).

Dougall, James Dalziell, *Salmon and Trout Angling.* Edinburgh and London, 1841.

Scottish Field Sports: a Volume of Mingled Gossip and Instruction. Edinburgh and London, 1861.

Dougall, John, *Angling Songs and Poems, with Miscellaneous Pieces.* Glasgow, 1901.

Dryden, Adam, *Hints to Anglers.* Edinburgh, 1862.

Edwards-Moss, John E, *A Season in Sutherland.* London, 1888.

'Ellangowan' (see Bertram, J G)

Ex-President of the Kinross-shire Fishing Club (see Begg, R B)

Ferguson, James R and Malcolm, *The Versatile Scot, also Fishing Adventures.* Stirling, 1911.

Fernie, Frederick, *Dry Fly Fishing in Border Waters.* London, 1912.

Fishing Gazette, *Fishing Gazette.* London (ed. R B Marston), 1–7 annually (1877–1883), thereafter two volumes per year, until 1966.

Ford, James A, *The Famed Midlothian Anglers. A Short History of the Midlothian Angling Association.* Edinburgh, 1984.

Forsyth, William, ('William O' Ye West'), *A Lay of Loch Leven.* Glasgow, 1877.

Fisherman's Magazine and Review, *Fisherman's Magazine and Review.* London (ed. H C Pennell), 1864 1, (only one volume published)

Francis, Francis, *A Book on Angling: Being a Complete Treatise on the Art of Angling in every Branch.* London, 1867–1920. (last edited by Sir Herbert Maxwell).

By Lake and River; an Angler's Rambles in the North of England and Scotland. London, 1874.

Franck, Richard, *Northern Memoirs . . . by Way of Dialogue.* London, 1694, 1821.

Fraser, Duncan, *Riverside Rambles of an Edinburgh Angler.* Selkirk, 1895, 1900.

Angling Songs from Border Streams. Selkirk, 1907.

Angling Sketches from a Wayside Inn. Edinburgh, 1911.

Gathorne-Hardy, Alfred E, *The Salmon.* London, 1898 (Longman, Green; Fur, Fin and Feather series).

Autumns in Argyleshire with Rod and Gun. London, 1900, 1901.

Geen, Philip, *What I have Seen while Fishing and How I have Caught my Fish.* London, 1905, 1924.

Days Stolen for Sport. London, 1907, 1914.

Gordon, Mary, *Memoir of Christopher North.* By his Daughter, Mrs Gordon. Edinburgh, 1862 (2 vols).

'Christopher North', a Memoir. Edinburgh, 1879 (2nd edition of preceding).

Grimble, Augustus, *Shooting and Salmon Fishing. Hints and Recollections.* London, 1892.

Highland Sport. London, 1894.
Leaves from a Game-Book. London, 1898.
The Salmon Rivers of Scotland. London, 1899, 1902, 1913.
Shooting and Salmon Fishing and Highland Sport. London, 1902.
Hall, Robert, *The Highland Sportsman.* Edinburgh and London, 1882–7 (annually).
Hamilton, Edward, *Recollections of Fly Fishing for Salmon, Trout and Grayling.* London, 1884, 1891.
Harvie-Brown, John A, *The Wonderful Trout.* Edinburgh, 1898.
Henderson, William, *Notes and Reminiscences of my Life as an Angler.* London, 1876, 1879, 1880.
Heywood, A, *One Way to the Tweed.* In Manchester Anglers' Association, 1882, 2, 17–29.
Hicks, James, *Wanderings by the Lochs and Streams of Assynt and North Highlands of Scotland.* London, 1855.
Hills, John Waller, *A History of Fly Fishing for Trout.* London, 1921–1973.
Hodge, Davies (? David) ('Yellow Body'), *Angling Days on Scotch Lochs.* Edinburgh and Dundee, 1884.
Hodgson, William Earl, *Trout Fishing.* London, 1904.
Salmon Fishing. London, 1906.
How to Fish. London, 1907.
An Angler's Season. London, 1903.
Hofland, Thomas C, *The British Angler's Manual . . . More Particularly for the Trout.* London, 1839.
Hutchinson, George Henry Hely ('Sixty-one'), *Twenty Years' Reminiscences of the Lews.* London, 1871, 1875.
Idle, Christopher, *Hints on Shooting and Fishing . . . of Christopher Idle Esq.* London, 1855.
Keill, James, *A Practical Treatise upon Angling . . . fishing in ponds.* Edinburgh, 1729.
Kelson, George M, *The Salmon Fly, How to Dress and How to Use It.* London, 1895.
Tips. London, 1901.
The Land and Water Salmon Flies, 1886–1902. Bovey Tracey, England, 1994.
Knox, Arthur E, *Autumns on the Spey.* London, 1872.
Knox, Robert, *Fish and Fishing in the Lone Glens of Scotland.* London and New York, 1854.
Lamond, Henry, *The Gentle Art, Some Sketches and Studies.* London, 1911.
A Mixed Basket. Paisley, 1914.
The Sea Trout. A Study in Natural History. London and Manchester, 1921a.
Some Piscatorial Problems Idly Considered. Manchester, 1921b.
Loch Lomond. A Study in Angling Conditions. Glasgow, 1931.
Days and Ways of a Scottish Angler. London, 1932.
Lang, Andrew, *Angling Sketches.* London, 1891, 1895.

Lawrie, William H, *Scottish Trout Flies. An Analysis and Compendium.* London, 1966.

Leech, John, *Mr Briggs and his Doings. Fishing.* London, 1861.

Leitch,A C, *A Scottish Fly Fisher.* Paisley, 1911.

Liddell, Robert, *The Lay of the Last Angler; or a Tribute to the Tweed at Melrose at the End of the Season of 1867.* Kelso, 1867, 1871, 1888 (under various titles).

Locke, James, *Tweed and Don; or Recollections and Reflections of an Angler for the last Fifty Years.* Edinburgh, 1860.

Lyall, J Watson, *The Sportsman's Tourist's and General Timetables and Guide to the Rivers, Lochs, Moors and Deer Forests of Scotland.* London, 1873–1915 (intermittently).

Mackenzie, J O, *Tweedside, with a Few Practical Hints.* In *Manchester Anglers' Association,* 1882, 2, pp. 30–43.

Mackie, Alexander, *The Art of Worm Fishing.* London, 1912.

MacVine, John, *Sixty-three Years Angling from the Mountain Streamlet to the Mighty Tay.* London, 1891.

McNee, James, *Trout Angling.* In *Fishing Gazette,* 1885, 10, 206, 243, 277, 288; 1885, 11, 218, 238.

Maitland, Sir James R G, *The History of Howietoun, Part 1.* Stirling, 1887.

Malloch, Peter D, *Salmon Flies and How to Make Them.* Bovey Tracey, England, 1994.

Manchester Anglers' Association, *Anglers' Evenings.* Manchester and London, 3 volumes: 1, 1880, 1883; 2, 1882; 3, 1894.

Maxwell, Sir Herbert E, *Salmon and Sea Trout: How to Propagate, Preserve and Catch Them in British Waters.* London, 1898.

Moffatt, A S, *The Secrets of Angling.* Edinburgh, 1865.

Morris, Wilfred W, *The Blameless Sport.* London, 1929.

An Angler in Arcadia. Edinburgh and London, 1934.

'North, Christopher' (see Wilson, John)

'Palmer Hackle' (see Blakey, Robert)

Pennell, Herbert Cholmondeley, *Fishing Gossip.* Edinburgh, 1866 (edited by HCP).

'Rainbow' (see Brown, W Sorley)

Robb, James, *Notable Angling Literature.* London, 1947.

Robertson, John, *Angling Streams and Angling Quarters in the Scottish Lowlands.* Edinburgh, 1859.

The Handbook of Angling for Scotland and the Border Counties. London, 1861.

Rooper, George, *Thames and Tweed.* London and New York, 1870, 1876, 1894.

St John, Charles, *Short Sketches of Wild Sport and Natural History of the Highlands.* Edinburgh, 1846–1948 (1919 edition edited by Sir Herbert Maxwell).

A Tour in Sutherlandshire. Edinburgh, 1849, 1884.

Scots Angler. A Monthly Magazine of River and Loch. Edinburgh, 1896–7 (edited by Andrew Smith).

Scrope, William, *Days and Nights of Salmon Fishing in the Tweed*. London, 1843, 1854, 1898, 1921 (last edited by H T Sheringham).

Simmonds, Norman W, *Man, I'm an Angler, Scots Magazine*, 1972, 98, pp. 120–6.

Man, I'm an Angler, Journal of the Flyfishers' Club, Summer 1994, 10–14.

'Sixty-One' (see Hutchinson, G H H)

Smythe, Patrick M, *The Diary of an All-round Angler*. London, 1956.

Speedy, Tom, *Sport in the Highlands and Lowlands of Scotland with Rod and Gun*. Edinburgh and London, 1884, 1886.

The Natural History of Sport in Scotland with Rod and Gun. Edinburgh and London, 1920.

Spence, Thomas F H, Wilson, R P and Other, A N ('Three Anglers'), *How to Catch Trout*. Edinburgh, 1888, 1889, 1902–1908.

Stewart, Tom, *Fifty Popular Flies and How to Tie Them*, Peterborough and London, 1962–73, (200 flies in four sets of 50).

Stewart, William Clouston, *The Practical Angler*. London, 1857, many editions and reprints to Centenary Edition, 1958, edited by W E Hodgson. Also illustrated facsimile of the first edition (1857) by Fly Fishers' Classic Library, Bovey Tracey, England, (1996).

Fly Fishing and How it Should be Done. In *Fishing Gossip*, ed. H C Pennell, 1866, pp. 291–306.

A Caution to Anglers. Edinburgh, 1871.

Stirling, John, *Andrew Smith. To his Memory*. Haddington, 1907.

Fifty Years with the Rod. With essays on What We Know of the Salmon and the Scottish Sea Trout. London, 1929.

Fishing for Trout and Sea Trout with Worm and Wet Fly. London, 1931.

Stoddart, Thomas Tod, *The Scottish Angler. The Art of Angling as Practised in Scotland*. Edinburgh, 1835, 1836.

Angling Reminiscences. Edinburgh, 1837.

The Angler's Companion to the Rivers and Lochs of Scotland. Edinburgh and London, 1847, 1853, 1892.

An Angler's Rambles and Angling songs. Edinburgh, 1866.

Rambles by Tweed. In *Fishing Gossip*, ed. H C Pennell, 1866, pp. 274–90.

Angling Songs. Edinburgh and London, 1889.

Stuart, Hamish, *Lochs and Loch Fishing*. London and Scarborough, 1899.

The Book of the Sea Trout, with some Chapters on Salmon. London, 1917, 1952 (edited by Rafael Sabatini).

Tait, John (see Anonymous), *Angler's Guide for the Shetlands*. Lerwick, 1903.

Thornton, Thomas, *A Sporting Tour through the Northern Parts of England and Great Part of the Highlands of Scotland*. London, 1804, 1806, 1896 (last edited by Sir Herbert E Maxwell).

'Three Anglers' (see Spence, Wilson and Other)

Tod, Ewen M, *Wet Fly Fishing Methodically Treated*. London, 1903, 1907, 1914, 1918.

Vannan, H, *Rambling Recollections of Fishing Days on the Aberdeenshire Don*. In *Manchester Anglers' Association*, 1882, 2, 210–42.

Walter, James C ('James Conway'), *Forays among Salmon and Deer*. London, 1861.

Recollections of Sport among Fin, Fur and Feather. London, 1885.

Webster, David, *The Angler and the Loop-Rod*. Edinburgh and London, 1885.

Westwood, Thomas, *A New Bibliotheca Piscatoria or General Catalogue . . . Notes and Data*. London, 1861.

Westwood, Thomas and Satchell, T, *Bibliotheca Piscatoria. A Catalogue of Books . . . Old English Authors*. London, 1883 (Revision of preceding entry; see also supplement by R B Marston, 1901).

'William O' Ye West' (see Forsyth, William)

Wilson, James, *The Rod and the Gun, being Two Treatises on Angling and Shooting*. Edinburgh, 1840, 1844.

Angling. Encyclopedia Britannica, ed. 7, 1842, pp. 3, 132–50.

Wilson, John ('Christopher North') *Noctes Ambrosianae*. Edinburgh, 1854; London and Glasgow, 1888; many others (selected reprints of papers from *Blackwood's Magazine*, bibliographically chaotic).

'Yellow Body' (see Hodge, Davies)

Young, Andrew, *The Angler's and Tourist's Guide to the Rivers, Lochs and Remarkable Places in the Northern Counties of Scotland*. Edinburgh, 1857, 1865.

Young, Archibald, *Angler's and Sketcher's Guide to Sutherland*. Edinburgh, 1880.

Younger, John, *River Angling for Salmon and Trout*. Kelso, 1840, 1860, 1864 (also 1994 in the Flyfisher's Classic Library, Bovey Tracey, England).

Index: People

Index: General